Jane Austen on Love

"Courtship," by Thomas Rowlandson

A watercolour of about 1786, in a private collection in England, reproduced by permission of the owner and of Phaidon Press, Limited.

JULIET McMASTER

Jane Austen on Love

English Literary Studies
University of Victoria

1978

© 1978 by Juliet McMaster

ELS Editions
Department of English
University of Victoria
Victoria, BC
Canada V8W 3W1
www.elseditions.com

Founding Editor: Samuel L. Macey

General Editor: Luke Carson

Printed by CreateSpace

No part of this publication may be reproduced, stored in a retrieval system or transmitted, in any form or by any means. Without the prior written consent of the publisher or a licence from The Canadian Copyright Licensing Agency (Access Copyright). For an Access Copyright licence, visit *www.accesscopyright.ca* or call toll free to 1–800–893–5777.

English literary studies monograph series
ISSN 0829-7681 ; 13
Includes bibliographical references.
ISBN-10 is 0-920604-24-2
ISBN-13 is 978-0-920604-24-3

CONTENTS

Texts and Abbreviations   6

Foreword   7

CHAPTER I   The Symptoms of Love   9

CHAPTER II   Surface and Subsurface   28

CHAPTER III   Love and Pedagogy   43

CHAPTER IV   Love and Marriage   63

Notes   81

TEXTS AND ABBREVIATIONS

References to Jane Austen's works are to R. W. Chapman's editions:

The Novels of Jane Austen, ed. R. W. Chapman, 5 vols, 3rd edition (London: Oxford University Press, 1932-4).

Minor Works, ed. R. W. Chapman (London: Oxford University Press, 1954).

Jane Austen's Letters to her Sister Cassandra and Others, ed. R. W. Chapman, 2nd edition (London: Oxford University Press, 1952).

E	Emma
Letters	Jane Austen's Letters to her Sister Cassandra and Others
MP	Mansfield Park
MW	Minor Works
NA	Northanger Abbey
P	Persuasion
PP	Pride and Prejudice
SS	Sense and Sensibility

FOREWORD

A graduate student in my course on the novel some years ago—she was better read though less guarded than many of her contemporaries—produced this critical comment after re-reading the chapters on Marianne's desertion by Willoughby in *Sense and Sensibility*: "Oh, Mrs. McMaster, I just cried and cried."[1] And a male colleague of mine once admitted that he found Elizabeth Bennet more sexually stimulating than the centre-fold of *Playboy*. I cite these two not altogether academic responses to Jane Austen's work as evidence for what will be my main arguments in the following chapters: that Jane Austen, knowing satirist and beautifully controlled comic artist though she is, is far from deficient in feeling; and that, notwithstanding her spinsterhood and her vaunted determination not to stray in subject-matter beyond the limits of her own experience, she is acutely awake to sex, and quite able to convey sexual feeling even though she may not take us into bedrooms.

Her novels are centrally concerned with courtship, and their culmination is marriage: for such a novelist Charlotte Brontë's contention that the Passions are perfectly unknown to her,[2] and Lawrence's strictures on her as an old maid "knowing in apartness,"[3] are serious charges. Yet the charges continue to reverberate—in the comic count of the total sixteen kisses in the six novels (none of them between a man and a woman), and in the popular conception of her as a writer whose most passionate encounters are conversations at a tea party or a walk to the vicarage.[4] Even many of her admirers are ready to admit that though she is a great novelist, it is not to Jane Austen that we should go if we want to be deeply moved: she is great for other reasons. I am ready to admit numbers of reasons for which she is a great novelist; but I find no need to apologise for her in the area of her main concern. My contention is that her subject was love, and she knew her subject.

CHAPTER I

The Symptoms of Love[1]

I'll begin by quoting Shakespeare's Rosalind, when she rebukes Orlando for looking so unlike a lover. The proper marks of a lover, she insists, are

> A lean cheek, which you have not; a blue eye and sunken, which you have not; ... a beard neglected, which you have not; but I pardon you for that. ... Then your hose should be ungarter'd, your bonnet unbanded, your sleeve unbutton'd, your shoe unti'd, and everything about you demonstrating a careless desolation. But you are no such man; you are rather point-device in your accoutrements.   (*As You Like It*, III, ii)

A lover, according to Rosalind, wears a uniform, by which you may know him. Rosalind has set herself up as an expert on the subject of love, and she cheerfully undertakes its diagnosis and cure.

For the moment I want to emulate Rosalind, and take it upon myself to explore some of the traditional scholarship on love, and some of the dramatizations of it, because Jane Austen, like Shakespeare in his comedies, makes love and the conventions surrounding it her subject. It is not just an emotion among others, it is a topic for debate, and for informed and playful commentary. Before I come to a consideration of the novels themselves, I will undertake a swift consideration of the Renaissance convention on love as Jane Austen inherited it. The subject, after all, has its own intrinsic interest.

Robert Burton's *Anatomy of Melancholy*, Dr. Johnson said, "was the only book that ever took him out of bed two hours sooner than he wished to rise."[2] Jane Austen is likely at least to have browsed in the favourite book of her favourite author; but she need not have known *The Anatomy of Melancholy* to have been familiar with much of the lore it contained. Many of the conventions and physical aberrations discussed in the fascinating section on Love Melancholy are still with us, as commonplaces of the behaviour of the lover. But I use Burton as my textbook, as he usefully collects the copious information on the subject.

Love melancholy is sexual love considered as a disease. "They that are in love are likewise sick," Burton states categorically (658).[3] The love malady has its physical causes and symptoms, its proper treatment and cure; and, if untreated, it is acknowledged as likely to end in death or the madhouse. "Go to Bedlam for examples," says Burton succinctly.

To speak first of its causes. The person of a sanguine temperament, whose blood predominates over the other humours of his body, is the most likely to fall victim to the love disease. A rich diet, strong wines, and a leisurely life, which promote the flux of blood, are apt to add to the predisposition to love. "Lascivious meats" and "Noble Wine first of all," says Burton, promote desire, and he adds one of his catalogues of inflammatory foods: "Honey mixtures, exquisite and exotick Fruits, Allspices, Cakes, Meat-broths, smoothly powerful wine...who would not then exceedingly rage with lust?... Inflammation of the belly is quickly worked off in venery, Hierome saith. After benching, then comes wenching" (663-4). Hence the modern lecher's refrain, "Have some Madeira, m'dear."

Sanguinity, youth, idleness and a rich diet create the predisposition to love. But the infection itself strikes from the sight of the beloved. When Phebe, Shakespeare's love-sick shepherdess, quotes Marlowe, "Who ever lov'd that lov'd not at first sight?" she is presenting the orthodoxy of the day. (By the way, Phebe, like another zealous advocate of first attachments, Marianne Dashwood, marries not her first love but her second.) Love happens all at once, it strikes like a thunderbolt, and it happens on the sight of the beloved. The meeting of the eyes is the crucial moment: from one pair of eyes to the other streaks a beam, or a ray, something that is conventionally represented as having a physical force, like Cupid's arrow; and then the victim is a goner. "Angry Cupid, bolting from her eyes, / Hath shot himself into me like a flame," moans Volpone. "Even so quickly may one catch the plague?" Olivia wonders in *Twelfth Night*; "Methinks I feel this youth's perfections, / With an invisible and subtle stealth / To creep in at mine eyes" (I, v). "The more [the lover] sees her," moralizes Burton, "the worse he is; the sight burns,... the rays of Love are projected from her eyes" (677). This love, "first learned in a lady's eyes," is an infection that proceeds, Burton says, through the vital spirits to the liver, heart, and finally the brain, so that it preoccupies appetite, passion and reason.[4] "The heart, eyes, ears, and all his thoughts are full of her," Burton explains. The progress to Bedlam has begun.

And now we come to the symptoms. On first taking the infection the lover stands bemused, he sighs, he is struck speechless, or if he speaks he speaks disconnectedly. The signs of falling in love become so formalised, in fact, that in one play Marston simply supplied the stage direction, "[*Isabella falls in love*],"[5] and left it to the actor to represent the condition to the audience's satisfaction.

Things go from bad to worse. The lover is sleepless. His pulse is uneven. After his indulgence in food and drink that made him prone to take the infection, he fasts. His total absorption in his love makes him affect solitude;

his infected reason makes his speech fragmentary; his interrupted respiration makes his breath come in gasps and sighs. Not surprisingly, he becomes pale and thin. Pallor is the badge of love—"Let everyone that loves be pale, for lovers 'tis the proper colour," Burton lays it down. Jacques Ferrand, author of a learned seventeenth-century work on *Erotomania*, further explains, "We must not understand by this word pale a simple decoloration or whiteness of the skin ... but rather a mixed colour of white and yellow; or of white, yellow and green."[6] Viola is therefore quite accurate in describing the state of her "sister" who died of love:

> She pin'd in thought
> And with a green and yellow melancholy
> She sat, like Patience on a monument,
> Smiling at grief.   (*Twelfth Night*, II, iv)

Those last lines, by the way, are among the tags from Shakespeare that Catherine Morland commits to memory (*NA*, 16).

It is necessary to distinguish between two forms of the love disease, the sanguine and the melancholic.[7] If the lover's suit is successful, his sanguine symptoms will continue, and he will blush and sing and be gay, and though he will be irrational in the idolatry of his beloved, his will not be a dangerous case for the physician. But the lover whose love is scorned turns from sanguine to melancholic; his blood corrupts to melancholy; and his sleeplessness and fasting wreak havoc with his constitution. Chaucer's Squire, with his embroidered tunic and cheerful music-making, is a classic example of the sanguine lover; but Arcite, in the Knight's Tale, is the pattern for the melancholic lover:

> His slep, his mete, his drynke, is hym biraft,
> That lene he wex, and drye as is a shaft;
> His eyen holwe, and grisly to biholde,
> His hewe falow, and pale as asshen colde,
> And solitarie he was and evere allone,
> And waillynge al the nyght, makynge his mone;
> And if he herde song or instrument,
> Thanne wolde he wepe, he myghte nat be stent.
> So feble eek were his spiritz, and so lowe,
> And chaunged so, that no man koude knowe,
> His speche nor his voys, though men it herde.   (1361-71)

In Jane Austen's novels, Mr. Elton is the type of the sanguine lover, with his fine display of symptoms, his blushing, sighing, and the charade on courtship, his own version of the classic lover's "ballad made to his mistress' eyebrow." Among the minor characters, Captain Benwick, at least before his cure, is Jane Austen's Arcite: he has "a melancholy air," we hear, "just as he ought to have, and drew back from conversation" (*P*, 97). The major character who displays all the classic symptoms of love melancholy is Marianne. The few paragraphs describing her condition after Willoughby's departure can stand as a parallel to the description of Arcite. In fact Marianne may well have had some such precedent in mind, for she does it all quite correctly. I quote selectively:

> She was awake the whole night, and she wept the greatest part of it. She got up with an headache, was unable to talk, and unwilling to take any nourishment.... When breakfast was over she walked out by herself,... indulging the recollection of past enjoyment and crying over the present reverse for the chief of the morning.... She played over every favourite song that she had been used to play to Willoughby,... and sat at the instrument gazing on every line of music that he had written out for her, till her heart was so heavy that no farther sadness could be gained.... She spent whole hours at the pianoforté alternately singing and crying; her voice often totally suspended by tears.... Such violence of affliction ... sunk within a few days into a calmer melancholy. (*SS*, 83)

According to the prosperity or ill success of his love, the lover's symptoms will vary. The careless desolation in dress, for instance, which Rosalind cites as the proper uniform of the lover, belongs to the melancholic phase of the disease. Had Rosalind had *The Anatomy of Melancholy* to hand, though, she might have been consoled to read, "let them be never so clownish, rude and horrid, Grobians and sluts, if once they be in love, they will be neat and spruce" (753). We, as an audience knowledgeable in the scholarship on love, can appreciate that Orlando is point-device in his accoutrements because his love is in fact a very prosperous one. He sees his beloved every day, though he does not know it. It is the kind of happy irony that Jane Austen loved as well as Shakespeare.

The symptoms in the classic lover's behaviour are manifold. If he really wants to do the thing properly he will wear a broad-brimmed hat over his eyes, and carry his arms folded. It is thus that the "Inamorato" is represented in the frontispiece to *The Anatomy of Melancholy*. So in *Love's Labour's Lost* Moth advises Don Armado that if he wants to convince discriminating wenches that he is in love, he must appear "with your hat penthouse-like o'er the shop of your eyes; with your arms cross'd on your thin-belly doublet like a rabbit on a spit" (III, i). Hence Berowne, another of Shakespeare's experts on love, calls Cupid "Regent of love-rhymes, lord of folded arms" (III, i). Compulsive versifying is also among the symptoms. "I do love; and it hath taught me to rhyme," admits Berowne.

The lover becomes particularly sensitive to the name of his beloved. Orlando packs Rosalind's name into every other line of verse, and carves it on all the trees; Cesario assures Olivia he will

> Halloo your name to the reverberate hills
> And make the babbling gossip of the air
> Cry out "Olivia!"   (*Twelfth Night*, I, v)

On the other hand the lover may become reticent about the name, and be unable to pronounce it, though he thinks it all the time. (Jane Austen's heroines usually belong in the latter category.)

The picture of the beloved is likewise sacred, and may prompt all the behavioural symptoms displayed on the first sight. By showing a picture the crafty physician may often diagnose a love malady, even if the patient is anxious to keep his love a secret. Proteus, in *The Two Gentlemen of Verona*, resolves to content himself with a picture *instead* of its original. He tells Silvia,

> Madam, if your heart be so obdurate,
> Vouchsafe me yet your picture for my love....
> To that I'll speak, to that I'll sigh and weep.   (IV, ii)

But the lover will dote not just on the portrait of the beloved, but on any image—such as a likeness perceived in the countenance of a relative; or any relic—such as a lock of her hair; or even, like Harriet Smith, the stub of a pencil or a piece of court plaister. When we hear, in an early chapter of *Emma*, that Mr. Knightley has preserved a reading list that Emma drew up when she was fourteen, we may draw our own conclusions (*E*, 37).

The lover's total absorption in his love makes him hypersensitive to the presence or approach of the loved one. "A lover's eyes will gaze an eagle blind," says Berowne. "She looks out at window still to see whether he come," says Burton. An updated Burton would include among his examples Elizabeth Bennet at the window of Longbourn, descrying before anyone else the figure of Darcy, and Anne Elliot in Bath, who can pick Wentworth out in a crowd at the far end of the street.

The physician who undertakes to cure a patient of the love disease can most easily treat the physical symptoms. His cures will correspond with the causes. To remedy the lover's sanguinity, bleed him;—the treatment of love was frequently a pretty gory business; to remedy his inflammatory rich diet, starve him, substituting a vegetable diet of "cowcumbers, melons,... Lettice" for the spicy foods; to remedy idleness, exercise him. A sixteenth-century French doctor, André Du Laurens, advises briskly, "Take away idleness, take away belly cheere, and quaffing of strong drinks, and without doubt lechery will fall stark lame."⁸ One can easily imagine why many a patient felt the cure was worse than the disease. And indeed this rather rigorous treatment, added to the symptoms of the melancholic lover, can bring the patient close to death's door. At this point, Burton advises humanely, "If they be much dejected and brought low in body, and now ready to despair through anguish, grief, and too sensible a feeling of their misery, a cup of wine ... is not amiss" (768).

But there are other cures, which have their different advocates. "I profess curing [love] by counsel," says Rosalind. The cure by good counsel involves the forceful representation of the irrationality of the patient's passion and of the defects of his beloved. But physicians admit that it seldom works. It is a sign that Elizabeth is not very far gone in love with Wickham that she takes her aunt's advice in such good part—"a wonderful instance," we hear, "of advice being given on such a point, without being resented" (*PP*, 145). More efficacious is what Burton calls the "contrary passion," or driving out one nail with another, and he quotes Ovid to the effect that "a new love thrusteth out the old" (776). But that can mean out of the frying pan, into the fire—like Romeo cured of Rosaline by Juliet, or Harriet Smith cured of Robert Martin by Mr. Elton.

"The last and best cure of Love-Melancholy," admits Burton at last, "is, to let them have their desire" (798). This may sound more like a total surrender to the disease than a treatment, but the wise physician is ready to consider marriage a prescription in order to free the lover from his pathological and irrational state of mind. Conjugal love is right and reasonable; and is offered as a sovereign cure to make "amantes no more amentes"— lovers no more madmen. So the physician and the comic dramatist unite in the final prescription of marriage, and many a successful case history, like many a romantic comedy, ends in a celebration of Hymen.

Jane Austen, like Shakespeare, both made fun of the love convention and used it. The earlier works, particularly, are full of high-spirited satire of all the commonplaces of love. Mr. Adams in *Jack and Alice* is "of so dazzling a Beauty that none but Eagles could look him in the Face." Alice is overpowered by "the Beams that darted from his Eyes," and instantly falls in love (*MW*, 13). In *Evelyn* the deserted Maria is "so much grieved at [her husband's] departure that she died of a broken heart about 3 hours after" (*MW*, 189). And the two heroines of *Love and Friendship* between them neatly fulfil the prognosis of the uncured love disease—Laura runs mad and Sophia dies (after imprudently fainting on the wet grass) (*MW*, 102). The young Jane is showing that she really shares Rosalind's unromantic doctrine:

"Men have died from time to time and worms have eaten them, but not for love" (*As You Like It*, IV, i). All this is good fun. But Jane Austen is ready to take love and its accepted conventions seriously too, to create her own Juliets and Cleopatras. In Marianne Dashwood she presents a girl who is so locked in to the convention that she almost dies in conforming to it; and our sympathies are fully engaged with Fanny Price and Anne Elliot, who suffer long and poignantly from the pangs of despised love.

The novels can be read as commentaries on the various controversies within the subject of love. Like the question of whether people can die of love, the convention of love at first sight and the issue of love's blindness come in for extended consideration, both within single novels and from one novel to another.

Marianne Dashwood is an ardent believer in the exclusive authenticity of first attachments, and a practitioner of love at first sight. Her practice and her principles are questioned and overthrown in *Sense and Sensibility*, and they are at issue too in the other works. In *Jack and Alice,* Lady Williams condoles with Alice on "the miseries, in general attendant on a first Love," and having experienced them herself, sensibly determines never to have a first love again (*MW*, 16). Isabella Thorpe, who does all her Love and Friendship by the book, assures Catherine, "So it always is with me; the first moment settles every thing. The first day that Morland came to us last Christmas—the very first moment I beheld him—my heart was irrecoverably gone" (*NA*, 118). But Isabella's heart proves to be more recoverable than she claims. *Pride and Prejudice,* with its theme of the unreliability of First Impressions, continues to reject the love at first sight convention in the main plot, but in the subplot of Bingley and Jane we have something close to the romantic pattern: "Oh! she is the most beautiful creature I ever beheld!" exclaims Bingley at the first ball (*PP*, 11); and all might have proceeded simply to swift marriage, but for outside interference. If the early novels value sense above sensibility, and a love based on esteem rather than instantaneous passion, *Persuasion* returns to something like the romantic ideal. Anne and Wentworth don't fall in love quite at first sight, but once acquainted, they are "rapidly and deeply in love" (*P*, 26). And Anne's first love is to be also her only love.

"Love is blind" is a proposition that is similarly debated. Cupid's blindness is supposedly communicated to the lover, who, on being smitten by the arrow, loses his power to see the defects of his beloved. Marianne, a vigorous adherent to the doctrine, "honoured her sister for [her] blind partiality" in not seeing Edward's shortcomings (*SS*, 19). *Emma* includes a prolonged exploration of the question of judgement and partiality in the lover. Emma's own conviction that love is blind is the source of many of her blunders: If Mr. Elton can talk of Harriet's "ready wit" he *must* be in love; on the other hand, since Mr. Knightley proves himself so thoroughly cognizant of her own faults, he must be in love with someone else. We are often invited to judge the state of a character's feelings by the degree of his appreciation for a lady's performance. Edward admires Elinor's drawings "as a lover, not as a connoisseur" (*SS*, 17); we are apprised of Colonel Brandon's rational passion for Marianne by the fact that at her piano recital "he paid her only the compliment of attention" (35). Emma is at last alerted to the real direction of Mr. Elton's attentions when he keeps "admiring her drawings with so much zeal and so little knowledge as seemed terribly like a would-be lover" (*E*, 118). "What you do / Still betters what is done," he would be understood to say, like some drawing-room Florizel (*The Winter's Tale*, IV, iv). And when Sir Walter Elliot is so impressed by Mrs. Clay's judicious use of Gowland's Lotion that he quite loses sight of her freckles, we know that he is far gone indeed.

Though Shakespeare and his contemporaries used the love convention, they were also so aware of its conventionality that they sometimes sought to express love in unconventional terms: so they created what we might call the anti-convention convention. "My mistress' eyes are nothing like the sun," declares this revolutionary in the realm of love. He rejects the convention in order to achieve a new immediacy, a greater authenticity in his expression. *Sense and Sensibility*, I think, is an extended essay in this genre. Marianne's is the conventional love, conceived at first sight, prompting heady joys and excessive manifestations, leading to desperation and almost to death. Elinor's is the love that is restrained in its expression, and hence it is invested with that pent-up energy that Shakespeare and Wyatt achieve in their anti-Petrarchan lyrics. It is a dangerous game to play, for it may come about that Marianne's histrionic displays capture our sympathy instead of Elinor's intense reticence. But it *can* succeed. In the novels at large, I think, Jane Austen does achieve a kind of muted intensity that can be as moving as more overtly passionate novels. But I shall have more to say of this in the next chapter.

We hear of Mrs. Dashwood at the beginning of *Sense and Sensibility* that "No sooner did she perceive any symptom of love in [Edward's] behaviour to Elinor, than she considered their serious attachment as certain" (17). Mrs. Dashwood is only one of a number of characters in the novels who are on the lookout for symptoms of love. And the symptoms are there all right, external signs, legitimate evidence that may be perceived and interpreted by the attentive observer. It is one of the conveniences of the love convention that it externalises emotion, and so enlarges the action, the working out of a love between two people, beyond the principals.

The accurate diagnosis of love is of major import in the plots of Jane Austen's novels. Consider *Pride and Prejudice*, for example. Bingley and Jane fall in love, and Bingley makes no secret of his admiration. When Jane is convalescing at Netherfield, "He was full of joy and attention. The first half hour was spent in piling up the fire, lest she should suffer from the change of room.... He then sat down by her, and talked scarcely to any one else. Elizabeth ... saw it all with great delight" (54). Elizabeth later speaks as a skilled diagnostician of love: "I never saw a more promising inclination. He was growing quite inattentive to other people, and wholly engrossed by her.... At his own ball he offended two or three young ladies, by not asking them to dance, and I spoke to him twice myself, without receiving an answer. Could there be finer symptoms? Is not general incivility the very essence of love?" (141). Mrs. Bennet is exultant, perceiving by such signs that Bingley is almost caught. But Darcy has been on the watch too. "I observed my friend's behaviour attentively; and I could then perceive that his partiality for Miss Bennet was beyond what I had ever witnessed in him" (197). Darcy regards Bingley's attachment to a girl of such connections as scarcely short of an illness, and he takes on the task that in Burton's day would have been the physician's, a cure of the malady by good counsel: "I readily engaged in the office of pointing out to my friend, the certain evils of such a choice.—I described, and enforced them earnestly" (198). However, as a man of honour Darcy does not proceed with detaching Bingley from Jane without attempting to ascertain first that the lady will not be seriously wounded by the rupture. He brings his diagnostician's eye to bear on Jane too:

> Your sister I also watched.—Her look and manners were open, cheerful and engaging as ever, but without any symptom of peculiar regard, and I remained convinced from the evening's scrutiny, that though she received his attentions with pleasure, she did not invite them by any participation of sentiment. (197)

Elizabeth at first rejects his claim to have taken pains to deduce Jane's feelings, but presently remembers that his testimony is corroborated by Charlotte Lucas, who had noted Jane's apparent serenity with uneasiness. Indeed, Bingley would not have been cured by Darcy's good counsel alone, but the assurance of Jane's indifference does end his courtship; at least until his physician, who has meanwhile been smitten by the same malady, prescribes the final cure—"to let them go together" and be married.

So the love of Jane and Bingley, which in itself would be a matter private to themselves, radiates outwards, by means of the external signs of love, to become a matter hotly at issue between the novel's two main characters. And the moral judgement on Darcy and Elizabeth must depend to some extent on their skill as diagnosticians of love.

The novels abound with such characters. Mrs. Jennings in *Sense and Sensibility* is one of the liveliest, though not always the most discriminating. "She was full of jokes and laughter, and before dinner was over had said many witty things on the subject of lovers and husbands." "She was remarkably quick in the discovery of attachments, ... and this kind of discernment enabled her soon after her arrival at Barton decisively to pronounce that Colonel Brandon was very much in love with Marianne Dashwood" (*SS*, 34, 36). As coming in the fourth chapter, that's an early and accurate diagnosis.

In her benevolent enterprise, once her daughters are off her hands, "to marry all the rest of the world" (36), Mrs. Jennings is a precursor of Emma, the character in all the novels who most prides herself on her skill in the diagnosis, cure, and promotion of love. She even contemplates "a Hartfield edition of Shakespeare," where she intends to add a long note of qualification to the proposition that "The course of true love never did run smooth" (*E*, 75). She presides, of course, mainly over Harriet's love life: she cures her by "good counsel" of her love for Robert Martin, talks her into love with Mr. Elton (and then finds she can't talk her out again so quickly), and benignly tolerates her symptoms of love for Frank Churchill. Besides that, she is quick to discover Jane Fairfax's illicit passion for Mr. Dixon (Mr. Dixon, after all, admired Jane's piano-playing more than his fiancée's— nothing could be clearer!). Emma gets it all wrong, of course. She misreads the symptoms, but the symptoms are there, and Mr. Knightley is attentive enough to discover something of the secret love of Jane and Frank.

Some of the women in the novels are put to the pain of diagnosing the symptoms in the men they love themselves. Fanny must watch Edmund's growing love for Mary Crawford, and Anne Elliot must speculate on the degree of attachment between Wentworth and the Musgrove girls: "Other opportunities of making her observations could not fail to occur. Anne had soon been in company with [them] often enough to have an opinion ... that Captain Wentworth was not in love with either. They were more in love with him; yet there it was not love. It was a little fever of admiration; but it might, probably must, end in love with some" (*P*, 82). Anne's skill is such that she can make these minute discriminations accurately.

For a character like Marianne, falling in love is as immedate and perceptible as for a figure in Renaissance comedy. The process is, after all, laid down in advance. When Willoughby rescues her, and carries her off, sprained ankle and all, to her home, she blushes profusely, is unable to speak, and, as soon as she casts an eye on his manly beauty, she is convinced that "of all manly dresses a shooting-jacket was the most becoming" (*SS*, 43). But other heroines do not have such ready access to their own emotions. Elizabeth and Emma are unconsciously in love with Darcy and Knightley before they ever detect themselves in the fact, and both even imagine themselves in love with other men. Everyone knows that even the best doctors are poor practitioners in their own cases, and so with such patients it is the reader who must become the diagnostician.

We, like Mrs. Jennings and the others, must read for symptoms. It is one of the great pleasures of reading the novels—much more fun than combing for clues in a detective novel. Emma, reflecting on the iniquities of Mrs. Elton in a long soliloquy, thus takes her own pulse: "Oh! what would Frank Churchill say to her, if he were here? How angry and how diverted he would be! Ah! there I am—thinking of him directly. Always the first person to be thought of! How I catch myself out!" (*E*, 279). The close reader, however, by looking back to the beginning of the soliloquy, will note that the "first person to be thought of" was actually Mr. Knightley, not Frank Churchill at all.

So it is with Elizabeth, who so singles out Darcy as an object of prejudice. In observing other lovers she is shrewd enough: when she meets Bingley in Derbyshire she can see the symptoms of his lasting feeling for Jane: "Sometimes she could fancy, that he talked less than on former occasions, and once or twice pleased herself with the notion that as he looked at her, he was trying to trace a resemblance" (*PP*, 262). But it is left to the reader to make the proper interpretation of the same symptom in Elizabeth when she meets Lady Catherine, "in whose countenance and deportment she soon found some resemblance of Mr. Darcy" (162).[9] In learning to read such signs the reader becomes a latter-day anatomist of love, and at least as well qualified to edit a new edition of Burton as Emma to edit the Hartfield edition of Shakespeare.

The modern reader on the lookout for symptoms might at first glance suppose that Jane Austen is above the rather quaint Renaissance conception of love as a physical state. Burton's disquisitions on sanguinity, diet, and the state of the liver seem rather far-fetched for useful application to nineteenth-century novels. But the Renaissance physiology of love is still perceptible, even if only in a vestigial form. Mr. Elton, well wined and dined at the Randalls dinner, is equally well primed for love-making: "two moments of silence being ample encouragement for Mr. Elton's sanguine state of mind, he tried to take [Emma's] hand again" (*E*, 131). "Sanguine" is a term used here in a sense Burton would surely have approved. The randy Alice Johnson, who finds herself "somewhat heated by wine (no very uncommon case)," is of a bright red complexion, and suffers from a "disordered Head and Love-sick Heart" (*MW*, 15). The view that amorousness is determined by physical makeup is partly confirmed by the physique of Jane Austen's most susceptible girls. Notice that the ones who are likely victims of seducers are robust: Lydia is "stout, well-grown, ... with a fine complexion" and "high animal spirits," the largest of the Bennet girls although the youngest (*PP*, 8, 45). Georgiana Darcy, Wickham's other intended victim, is "tall, and on a larger scale than Elizabeth; and, though little more than sixteen, her figure was formed, and her appearance womanly" (*PP*, 261). The Bertram girls, both susceptible to the charms of Henry Crawford, are "tall, full-formed, and fair" (*MP*, 44). And Marianne, who resembles Colonel Brandon's fallen first love, is taller than Elinor, with a complexion "uncommonly brilliant" (*SS*, 46).

Burton's strictures on diet, too, still reverberate. It is surely no accident that Mr. Woodhouse is equally opposed to a rich diet and to matrimony! And Emma's present of arrowroot to Jane Fairfax, reminiscent of Burton's vegetable diets, is cruelly though unintentionally appropriate. No wonder Jane should resent a remedy of love contributed by her rival. Mrs. Jennings may well have used *The Anatomy of Melancholy* as her Home Doctor volume, for when Marianne has been deserted by Willoughby she presses Elinor to take her a glass "of the finest old Constantia wine." Elinor pleads that as Marianne has already fallen asleep she may drink it herself. After all, she reflects, "its healing powers on a disappointed heart might be as reasonably tried on herself as on her sister" (*SS*, 197-8). As Burton directed, if the lover is much dejected, "a cup of wine ... is not amiss."

The quickened pulse and consequent variation in complexion are further useful signs for the diagnostician, both in *The Anatomy of Melancholy* and in Jane Austen's novels. Burton cites one shrewd physician who was able to discover his patient was in love, and with whom, "by his Pulse and Countenance, ... because that when she came in presence, or was named, his pulse varied, and he blushed besides" (723). We may reach similar conclusions by observing the same signs in the novels. When she sees Willoughby in London, Marianne's face is first "glowing with sudden delight," then "crimsoned over," and presently she is "looking dreadfully white." Well may Elinor warn her lest she "betray what you feel to every body present" (*SS*, 176-7). In the later novels the signs are presented more subtly. When Edmund recounts his father's praises to a blushing Fanny—"Nay, Fanny, do not turn away about it—it is but an uncle"—the reader is aware of the irony of Edmund's missing a sign, for Fanny is "distressed by more feelings than he was aware of" (*MP*, 198). Anne at the beginning of *Persuasion* "hoped she had outlived the age of blushing" (49), but it is among the signs of her emotional regeneration and her physical rejuvenation that she is later to regain her "bloom" and the ability to blush. After the concert in Bath, where she was approached by Wentworth and overtly courted by Elliot, Mrs. Smith plays the role of the physician: "Your countenance perfectly informs me that you were in company last night with the person, whom you think the most agreeable in the world...." A blush overspread Anne's cheeks. She could say nothing" (194). The men blush too, though more frequently they "colour." There is one nicely veiled hint of Mr. Knightley's feelings when Emma suggests he may be in love with Jane Fairfax: "Mr. Knightley was hard at work upon the lower buttons of his thick leather gaiters, and either the exertion of getting them together, or some other cause, brought the colour into his face" (*E*, 287). Here he is blushing not at the mention of Jane Fairfax, but because it is Emma who suggests he is in love. Emma herself could hardly be expected to read this sign, but the reader is invited to. Emma works on such symptoms in her own misguided way. When Harriet has a cold, she tries to raise Mr. Elton's sensibility by this suggestive description of her condition: "a throat very much inflamed, with a great deal of heat about her, a quick low pulse, &c." Mr. Elton can only reply with the exasperating comment, "A sore-throat!—I hope not infectious" (109). After Elton's insult to Harriet at the ball, Emma draws the satisfaction that at least Harriet will have been cured of her love for him. "The fever was over, and Emma could harbour little fear of the pulse being quickened again" (332). What Emma doesn't know is that Harriet's volatile pulse has already been quickened again, by Mr. Knightley's stepping forward to save her from Mr. Elton's insult. So Jane Austen takes over a convention, uses it, shows how her characters use it, and makes her reader aware of its intricacies.

Though the gloomy prognosis of death or madness is not often fulfilled in Jane Austen's realistic novels, she does often show how a disappointed passion can have serious physical consequences. Marianne is a classic case of love melancholy. "It was many days since she had any appetite, and many nights since she had really slept, and ... the consequence of all this was felt in an aching head, a weakened stomach, and a general nervous faintness" (*SS*, 185). In her illness at Cleveland, which is almost fatal, her pulse is "lower and quicker than ever!" and she is feverish and delirious (311). Men who are crossed in love, like Edward Ferrars, Colonel Brandon, and

Captain Benwick, generally give themselves away by showing "oppression of spirits" (*SS*, 50, 90; *P*, 97). Even Mr. Knightley loses his physical vigour when he supposes Emma is about to marry Frank Churchill, and prompts the sad comment from his nieces and nephews, "Uncle seems always tired now" (*E*, 465). But the women are more definitely debilitated. Anne loses her bloom as well as her spirits when she breaks her engagement; Fanny's sick headache has as much to do with Edmund's attentions to Mary Crawford as with her picking roses in the sun; Jane Fairfax in Frank's absence suffers from "a weakened frame and varying spirits" (*E*, 166), and after their quarrel she is actually a case for the doctor. "Her health seemed for the moment completely deranged—appetite quite gone— ... her spirits seemed overcome" (389). Hers is a malady that Burton would recognize as being beyond any treatment but the last and final cure of marriage, which happily is forthcoming. As Mrs. Elton says knowingly, "Upon my word, Perry has restored her in a wonderful short time! ... We do not say a word of any *assistance* that Perry might have; not a word of a certain young physician from Windsor. [That is, Frank.]—Oh! no; Perry shall have all the credit" (*E*, 454). As for Frank himself, he claims—and means to be believed—that if Jane had refused him, "I should have gone mad" (437). Fortunately however the same sovereign remedy keeps him out of Bedlam.

The time-honoured convention of the force of the eyes, the exchange of looks between lovers, remains a strong influence in the novels. We hear much of the attractive power of the heroine's eyes on the hero—Catherine's "sparkling eyes" as she accepts Tilney's invitation to dance (*NA*, 75); "the beautiful expression of her dark eyes" that overcomes Elizabeth's other disadvantages in Darcy's estimation (*PP*, 23); Mary Crawford's "lively dark eye" that so charms Edmund, until he learns "to prefer soft light eyes to sparkling dark ones" (*MP*, 44, 470); and Emma's "true hazel eye" that makes Mr. Knightley "love to look at her" (*E*, 39). A good deal of significant action in the novels takes the form of exchanges of glances between lovers or would-be lovers. When Mr. Elton presents his charade, which prays conventionally, "May its approval beam in that soft eye!" Emma knows there are signs to be read, but misreads them: "There was deep consciousness about him, and he found it easier to meet her eye than her friend's" (*E*, 71). One longs to alert Emma to this clear sign that he is courting her, not Harriet. In other places, however, Emma can manage the *coup d'oeil* with some finesse—as at the ball with Mr. Knightley, where "her eyes invited him irresistibly to come to her" (330).

In *Persuasion* there is a whole history of looks between lovers. The estrangement between Anne and Wentworth is emphasised by their failure to meet each other's eyes: "Her eye half met Captain Wentworth's"—or—"*Once* she felt that he was looking at herself" (*P*, 59, 72). Only at Lyme, where she begins to recapture his attention, does she receive "a glance of brightness" (104) from him; their continuing misunderstanding in Bath is signalled again by their failure to manage glances: "As her eyes fell on him, his seemed to be withdrawn from her" (188); but at the last he places his letter of proposal before her "with eyes of glowing entreaty" (*P*, 236). "A word, a look will be enough to decide," he writes. And when they meet, in Union Street, Anne is able to give him the right look (238, 239). The progress of their relation is marked by averted eyes, intercepted glances, and at last the full exchange of loving looks.

In dress we have Marianne again as the conventional model, demonstrating the careless desolation of the melancholy lover: "To her dress and appearance she was grown... perfectly indifferent" (*SS*, 249)—unlike Miss Steele who, always in hope to catch the next beau, is point-device in her accoutrements. There are no broad-brimmed melancholy hats in evidence; but Harriet is able to see in "the very sitting of his hat,... proof of how much [Mr. Elton] was in love!" (*E*, 184).

Mr. Elton, who much enjoys the trappings of a lover, is likewise a heavy sigher. Even Emma, delighted as she is at his promising attachment to Harriet, becomes almost exasperated: "He does sigh and languish, and study for compliments rather more than I could endure as a principal" (*E*, 49). And the attentive reader who attunes his ear to sighs may gather almost as much as the one on the lookout for dialogues of eyes or quickenings of pulse.

It is of course *de rigueur* that the dedicated lover, like Chaucer's Squire, should "sleep namoore than dooth a nyghtyngale." Marianne, we hear, "would have thought herself very inexcusable had she been able to sleep at all the first night after parting from Willoughby" (*SS*, 83). Isabella Thorpe proudly exclaims to Catherine, "Oh, Catherine, the many sleepless nights I have had on your brother's account!" (*NA*, 118). So when Elizabeth after her visit to Pemberley "lay awake two whole hours" (265) trying to determine what are her feelings for Darcy, the reader could tell her the answer there and then, on the basis of the insomnia alone.

Shakespeare's pastoral lover, Silvius, makes unsociability and the courting of solitude a definitive symptom of love:

> If thou hast not broke from company,
> Abruptly, as my passion now makes me,
> Thou hast not lov'd.... [*Exit*]   (*As You Like It*, II, iv)

So Elizabeth lays it down, "Is not general incivility the very essence of love?"

(*PP*, 141). It takes Marianne several days, after Willoughby's departure, to bring herself to walk with her sisters "instead of wandering off by herself" (*SS*, 85); and indeed it is on one such solitary ramble that she contracts her putrid throat. Julia Bertram, when Henry Crawford has chosen her sister to play opposite him in the production of *Lovers' Vows*, sits apart "in gloomy silence, wrapt in such gravity as nothing could subdue" (*MP*, 160); and she and Fanny, both watching the amorous adventures of the Crawfords, are "two solitary sufferers." Fanny and Anne Elliot, both of whom are divided from their men through most of the action, are alike also characterized by their loneliness: for Anne, as for Fanny, "her own thoughts and reflections were habitually her best companions" (*MP*, 80). Indeed, the noticeable need of the heroine at times of stress to withdraw, and cope with her feelings in private, is Jane Austen's characteristic adaptation of the conventional lover's penchant for solitude. As Jane Fairfax says feelingly, after she has quarrelled with Frank, "Oh, Miss Woodhouse, the comfort of being sometimes alone!" (*E*, 363).

Viola in *Twelfth Night* is able to discover that Olivia has fallen in love by the fact that "she did speak in starts distractedly" (II, ii). Broken and confused speech is likewise a reliable symptom of love in Jane Austen's novels. Darcy's feelings for Elizabeth are deducible from his unconnected sentences and relapses into silence when he calls at the parsonage in Hunsford (*PP*, 177ff). Mr. Elton is again a model lover when he looks at Emma's painting and "sighed out his half sentences of admiration just as he ought" (*E*, 69). This is a specimen of Mr. Knightley's syntax when he believes Emma to have loved and lost Frank Churchill: "Her arm was pressed again, as he added, in a more broken and subdued accent, 'The feelings of the warmest friendship—Indignation—Abominable scoundrel!'" (426). Even Tilney can be inarticulate: on his visit to the Allens after his proposal, he "talked at random, without sense or connection" (*NA*, 243).

The time-honoured relation between the lover and the picture of his beloved is the basis of many a subtle incident involving pictures in Jane Austen's fiction. An early instance, in *Evelyn*, is the sad story of Rose Gower, who after losing her fiancé at sea, seeks "to soften her affliction by obtaining a picture of her unfortunate Lover" (*MW*, 185). The same incident recurs, with subtle expansion to include the question of constancy in men and women, in *Persuasion*, where Benwick's picture, painted for Fanny Harville, is to be reframed for his new fiancée, Louisa Musgrove. Elizabeth at Pemberley re-enacts the classic lover's reaction to the portrait, but in a movingly updated version. She wanders through the gallery until she finds what she is looking for, Darcy's portrait:

> At last it arrested her—and she beheld a striking resemblance of Mr. Darcy, with such a smile over the face, as she remembered to have sometimes seen, when he looked at her. She stood several minutes before the picture in earnest contemplation. (*PP*, 250)

Burton would have signed her up for emergency treatment at once.

The complex muddle over Mr. Elton's admiration of Emma's portrait of Harriet shows that Emma has got her conventions confused. Mr. Elton is determined to be a conventional lover, and Emma is determined to read the conventional signs. But he is flashing the "Everything you do is perfect" sign, while Emma is receiving the "Lover doats on portrait" message. Hence she takes Harriet to be his object, not herself. It is a beautiful play with the love convention.

The sound of the name of the beloved can be almost as dangerous as his picture or his actual presence. Elinor helps Marianne in her extremity by avoiding the mention of Willoughby: "Her carefulness in guarding her sister from ever hearing Willoughby's name mentioned, was not thrown away" (*SS*, 214). Catherine, as she is expelled from Northanger Abbey, stammers to Eleanor Tilney " 'her kind remembrance for her absent friend.' But with this approach to his name ended all possibility of restraining her feelings" (*NA*, 229). Such reaction being the convention, sharper ladies than Catherine become self-conscious about the matter. Mary Crawford writes to Fanny in Portsmouth, "Of [your cousin Edmund], what shall I say? If I avoided his name entirely, it would look suspicious" (*MP*, 416). Naturally, our suspicions are simultaneously raised and confirmed. And Emma, always taking her own pulse to measure her love for Frank Churchill, goes through this palpitating soliloquy:

> Am I unequal to speaking his name at once before all these people? Is it necessary for me to use any roundabout phrase? ... No, I can pronounce his name without the smallest distress. I certainly get better and better.— Now for it ... Mr. Frank Churchill writes one of the best gentlemen's hands I ever saw. (*E*, 297)

The reader can smile knowingly as Emma waits in suspense to feel the symptoms of a disease she doesn't have.

Except for Mr. Elton's charade, the lover's inclination to versify is not abundantly demonstrated in Jane Austen's novels. In fact Elizabeth pointedly suggests that writing poetry is the cure of love, rather than its symptom. "I wonder who first discovered the efficacy of poetry in driving away love!" she says (*PP*, 44), anticipating the unromantic view of her descendant, Thackeray, who similarly suggested, "when a gentleman is cudgelling his brain to find any rhyme for sorrow, besides borrow and to-morrow, his woes are nearer at an end than he thinks for" (*Pendennis*, Ch. 15). But an indulgence in music is still a proper activity for a lover, and Marianne, in playing over all the songs she has sung with Willoughby, is like that other orthodox lover, Orsino in *Twelfth Night*, who exclaims, "If music be the food of love, play on!"

"But," says Burton, as he is struggling to an end of his section on Symptoms, "I conclude there is no end of Love's Symptoms, 'tis a bottomless pit" (761). Emma, another expert on the subject, likewise acknowledges, "There may be a hundred different ways of being in love" (*E*, 49)—though she is confident that she is mistress of them all.

I proceed then to the cures. Blood-letting, as Wordsworth's leech-gatherer testifies, is no longer fashionable, but dieting has not quite disappeared: as I have said, Mr. Woodhouse undertakes to cure all and sundry before they ever sicken by a steady diet of coddled eggs and gruel. The cure by good counsel is attempted on Catherine Morland by her mother, on Bingley by Darcy, on Harriet by Emma (more than once), and on Anne by Lady Russell. It never works. The cure of the contrary passion is confirmed as more successful. Mrs. Jennings professes this cure and almost quotes Burton—"one shoulder of mutton, you know, drives another down" (*SS*, 197); and indeed her prescription is successful, as Marianne is ultimately cured of Willoughby by Brandon. A "second attachment," we know, would be "the only thoroughly natural, happy, and sufficient cure" (*P*, 28) for Anne's wounded heart but that she manages to resuscitate the first attachment. And successive attachments are the only treatment for Harriet's almost chronic state of lovesickness: "The charm of an object to occupy the many vacancies of Harriet's mind was not to be talked away. [Mr. Elton] might be superseded by another ... but nothing else ... would cure her" (*E*, 183-4). However, with Burton, Jane Austen finally prescribes the treatment of marriage, and a highly acceptable one it is. She, like Shakespeare, writes romantic comedies, after all.

A number of modern critics have shown us Jane Austen as the novelist of "regulated hatred," as the bitter satirist, as a writer with almost tragic reach. I have preferred for the moment to dwell on her affinities with Shakespearean comedy, because Jane Austen is a novelist who also celebrates joy and consummation. For all her restraint in depicting sexuality, she can reach like Shakespeare to delight—exuberantly, jubilantly—in the joy of love requited. "O coz, coz, coz, my pretty little coz," exclaims Rosalind in her happiness, "that thou didst know how many fathom deep I am in love!" (IV, i). We find similar jubilant, sparkling passages in the novels. "I am happier even than Jane," says Elizabeth; "she only smiles, I laugh" (*PP*,

383). Or, when Wentworth agrees to escort Anne home in Bath: "There could be only the most proper alacrity, a most obliging compliance for public view; and smiles reined in and spirits dancing in private rapture" (*P*, 240). How many fathom deep they are in love!

Jane Austen's romantic comedies are close to Shakespeare's not just in their playful treatment of the conventions of love, but sometimes in the deliberate choice of situations through which to explore the intricate pains and pleasures of love. As I shall show in more detail in later chapters, Elizabeth Bennet is a descendant of Beatrice in *Much Ado*: both of them single out their men for pointed abuse before a happy reconciliation. Fanny Price is a latter-day Viola, constrained to the painful task of being the go-between in the suit of the man she loves for another woman. And Emma Woodhouse, who takes on the arrangement of other people's love lives while her own is in jeopardy, is a version of Rosalind.

"I believe in a true analogy between our bodily frames and our mental," says Captain Harville (*P*, 233)—a proposition which Anne, and Jane Austen too, accept. From the old conception of the humours, the theory that character derives from physical constitution, Jane Austen inherited a sense that love is not just a state of mind, but a state of body. To the intelligent observer its signs are as definite and palpable as a rash or a high temperature. For us moderns, who use what we call intuition to divine the state of each others' hearts, she would have a tolerant compassion—we are so many Mrs. Dashwoods and unreformed Emmas, relying on inspired guesses that may just as likely be wrong as right. And those outward and visible signs of love serve her purpose as a novelist, too. The artist must deal in appearances, and the visible symptoms of love—its language, as it were—are a fine ready-made set of terms by which to communicate its reality. Jane Austen writes for a reader who is "in the lore / Of deep love learned to the red heart's core."[10] The phrase is Keats's, but the sentiment fits. As her characters are scholars of love, so must we be.

CHAPTER II

Surface and Subsurface[1]

I take the metaphor of my chapter title from Charlotte Brontë's memorable criticism of Jane Austen:

> She does her business of delineating the surface of the lives of genteel English people curiously well; there is a Chinese fidelity, a miniature delicacy in the painting: she ruffles her reader by nothing vehement, disturbs him by nothing profound: the Passions are perfectly unknown to her; she rejects even a speaking acquaintance with that stormy Sisterhood; ... Her business is not half so much with the human heart as with the human eyes, mouth, hands and feet; what sees keenly, speaks aptly, moves flexibly, it suits her to study, but what throbs fast and full, though hidden ... —*this* Miss Austen ignores.[2]

It is the original and recurring objection to Jane Austen. Mark Twain (who apparently so missed violence in the novels that he thought she shouldn't have been allowed to die a natural death![3]), complained that her characters are automatons which can't "warm up and feel a passion."[4] And even her admirers defended her in terms which to her detractors are damningly faint praise. George Henry Lewes announced, "First and foremost let Jane Austen be named, the greatest artist that has ever written, using the term to signify the most perfect mastery over the means to her end. There are heights and depths in human nature which Miss Austen has never scaled nor fathomed, there are worlds of passionate existence into which she has never set foot; ... Her circle may be restricted, but it is complete."[5] Elizabeth Barrett Browning was all too ready to accept this view: the novels, she said, are "perfect as far as they go—that's certain. Only they don't go far, I think."[6] "Perfect," for Mrs. as for Mr. Browning, is a term of opprobrium. It means the reach doesn't exceed the grasp.

In the twentieth century Jane Austen certainly does not want for discriminating critics who make large claims for her significance, but again we who are her admirers have taken our stand on her appeal to the head rather than the heart. Ian Watt quotes Horace Walpole's dictum that "this world is a comedy to those that think, a tragedy to those that feel," and acknowledges "Jane Austen's novels are comedies, and can have little appeal to those who, consciously or unconsciously, believe thought inferior to feeling."[7] We have to a large extent conceded Charlotte Brontë's point, and agreed that Jane Austen's business is indeed with the head and not with the heart—we simply don't find her reaction as devastating a piece of criticism as she evidently meant it to be: valuing as we do the activity of the mind and the application of the intellect. We admire the unruffled surface, and have a properly Augustan reservation about the virtues of the kind of "vehemence" and "profundity" that Brontë misses.[8] I myself have just been demonstrating Jane Austen's intellectual savouring of the love convention, and her affinities with Shakespearean comedy.

And yet... do we really need to concede as much as we do? In our heart of hearts (and I use the phrase designedly) don't we know that a *full* reading of a Jane Austen novel is a very *moving* experience, as well as an intellectually delectable one?—that the moment of reconciliation when Mr. Knightley *almost* kisses Emma's hand is fraught with passion, just as is the occasion when Mr. Rochester crushes Jane Eyre to his breast in the orchard at Thornfield, while a violent midsummer storm is brewing?

How is it done? Well, deep reservoirs may have unruffled surfaces as well as shallow ones: if unruffled surface is what we admire, then we need not look beyond it—and we can delight in the fidelity with which the surface of the lives of genteel English people is delineated; but if we do indeed value the dramatization of deep emotion, that too is there, and the more visible, if not the more obvious, for the apparent tranquillity.

Charlotte Brontë, accused on one occasion of equivocation, vindicated herself vigorously: "I would scorn in this and every other case to deal in equivoque; I believe language to have been given us to make our meaning clear, and not to wrap it in dishonest doubt."[9] I suspect Jane Austen would consider such a declaration somewhat crude. The naïve Catherine Morland in *Northanger Abbey* has something similar to say of General Tilney's white lies: "Why he should say one thing so positively, and mean another all the while, was most unaccountable! How were people, at that rate, to be understood?" (*NA*, 211). And Catherine's education is to involve the realization that language need not always be interpreted literally.

Of course novelists and dramatists have traditionally made capital out of a discrepancy between the profession and the reality, and many a comic scene has been built around it. Here is Becky Sharp, justifying herself to Jos Sedley when he has come to visit her in her disreputable lodgings: she has just stowed the brandy bottle, the rouge-pot, and the plate of broken meat in the bed.

"I have had so many griefs and wrongs, Joseph Sedley, I have been made to suffer so cruelly, that I am almost made mad and sometimes.... I had but one child, one darling, one hope, one joy, which I held to my heart with a mother's affection ... ; and they—they tore it from me—tore it from me;" and she put her hand to her heart with a passionate gesture of despair, burying her face for a moment on the bed.

The brandy-bottle inside clinked up against the plate which held the cold sausage. Both were moved, no doubt, by the exhibition of so much grief. (*Vanity Fair*, Ch. 65)

Becky pours out her wrongs and her griefs; the brandy bottle and the rouge-pot tell a different story. Sometimes Thackeray even provides a direct translation of the subsurface meaning. In another memorable scene between the same pair, when they nervously await the event of Waterloo in Brussels, Becky tells Jos:

"You men can bear anything. . . . Parting or danger are nothing to you. Own now that you were going to join the army and leave us to our fate. I know you were—something tells me you were. I was so frightened, when the thought came into my head (for I do sometimes think of you when I'm alone, Mr. Joseph!), that I ran off immediately to beg and entreat you not to fly from us."

This speech might be interpreted, "My dear sir, should an accident befall the army, and a retreat be necessary, you have a very comfortable carriage, in which I propose to take a seat." (Ch. 31)

I have indulged in this little digression on Becky Sharp because she provides a convenient contrast to the usual process in Jane Austen. Becky's speech is a gush of emotion; Becky's meaning is totally a product of that energetic brain of hers, and one can almost hear the whirr and click of a calculating machine in action. Jane Austen's characters, on the other hand, conduct apparently rational conversations with each other on subjects of general interest, while simultaneously their *hearts* are deeply engaged. She is not particularly interested in the exposure of the hypocrite who uses social forms as a mask for his true motivation.[10] Nor is Charlotte Brontë, by the way—it is notable that in the proposal scene in *Jane Eyre* Jane declares explicitly, "I am not talking to you now through the medium of custom, [or] conventionalities" (Ch. 23). Jane Eyre and Lucy Snowe have to maintain a proud reticence, or burst through the barriers of convention in order to express their feelings, and when they do burst through they mean all they say; Becky Sharp and Blanche Amory are socially perfectly at ease in the display of emotion, but they mean something different. But Jane Austen's characters succeed in expressing themselves not in spite of custom and convention, but *through* them; and they mean not something different from what they say, like Thackeray's, nor all they say, like Charlotte's, but far more than what they say. So when Elinor receives Edward after their estrangement, actually believing him to be married to Lucy Steele, we can gather enough of the agonized state of her feelings by hearing merely that "she sat down again and talked of the weather" (*SS*, 359).

And here we come to her powerful use of understatement in emotional scenes. It is her frequent practice to bring a situation to a crisis, to lead you to the point where you expect some climactic exclamation of the "Great was her consternation...!" type, and then to report instead some apparent commonplace of behaviour or polite converse. There is a breath of a pause, a kind of hiatus between cause and effect (which I indicate typographically by a double stroke), that we learn to perceive and savour. "No sooner had Fatima discovered the gory remains of Bluebeard's previous wives, // than she made an appointment with her hairdresser"—I must invent a gross example to attune the ear and eye to Jane Austen's refined and delicate use of this device.

For instance:

Elizabeth Bennet has at last realized that Darcy is the man she loves, but just when she has come to believe that he will never approach her again. Her mother calls her to the window to see the arrival of Mr. Bingley. "Elizabeth, to satisfy her mother, went to the window—she looked,—she saw Mr. Darcy with him, and // sat down again by her sister" (*PP*, 333).

Mary Crawford, in spite of her prejudice against younger brothers, has fallen in love with Edmund Bertram. She is engaged in a game of Speculation when the gentlemen's conversation turns on the eligibility of Thornton Lacy as a gentleman's residence: "Thornton Lacey was the name of [Edmund's] impending living, as Miss Crawford well knew; and // her interest in a negociation for William Price's knave increased" (*MP*, 241).

Anne Elliot has steeled herself to speak to Mrs. Croft of her brother, Captain Wentworth, brave in the knowledge that Mrs. Croft knows nothing of the previous engagement:

> "Perhaps you may not have heard that he is married," added Mrs. Croft.
> [Anne] // could now answer as she ought.   (*P*, 49)

Again and again Jane Austen indicates a severe emotional shock by this kind of understatement. She is not *avoiding* the presentation of strong feelings; she is presenting them by indirection. It is not because her characters have no feelings that they talk of the weather and make polite responses in such moments. Words would not carry the full weight of what they feel in any case. They observe the social forms, but not at the expense of crushing themselves. For what they feel they *can* express, but they can seldom express it directly or fully: to spill out the words and feelings, regardless of decorum, is to lose the intensity, to be emotionally shallow. (That is what Jane Austen tried to suggest in *Sense and Sensibility,* when Elinor hears the man she loves is married, and *Marianne* goes into hysterics.) Her people speak in a succinct code, where A expresses not only A, but B and C as well.

I would like to examine, in some detail, a few passages of dialogue, and to show how polite conversation, conducted on matters of apparently general import, and within the bounds of decorum, can be informed with a subsurface level of intense personal emotion. One thing is said on the surface; but below the surface are implied the individual's ecstasies and agonies. In this way I hope to mine some of that rich and primitive ore which Charlotte Brontë misses.[11]

I will confine myself to the last three novels, partly for convenience (one has to stop somewhere), but also because I think that this is an aspect of Jane Austen's art which she developed and refined, and used with best effect later in her career. Lucy Steele's bitchy insinuations in *Sense and Sensibility* are relatively crude examples of a character's ability to suggest more than is stated, compared with Frank Churchill's elaborate *doubles entendres,* or with the kind of oblique communication that constantly goes on between Anne Elliot and Captain Wentworth, where, though they seldom speak to each other, each constantly understands the full import of the other's speech better than their interlocutors do. In my selection of passages I deliberately choose situations that parallel Charlotte Brontë's characteristic one, where the protagonist is forced to look on while the man she loves is courting an unworthy rival: a Blanche Ingram or a Ginevra Fanshawe, a Mary Crawford or a Louisa Musgrove. In such situations Jane Austen puts her reader on stage, as it were, since we become with the protagonist spectators who are intimately aware of unspoken implications in the exchanges we witness.

My first extract is from the famous excursion to Sotherton in *Mansfield Park.* Mary Crawford, Edmund and Fanny, the trio who are so constantly associated, have begun to wander in the little "wilderness" of the park. Mary has just heard that Edmund is to take orders, and has had all her prejudices against younger brothers renewed. "A clergyman is nothing," she declares. Edmund defends his vocation.

> "A clergyman cannot be high in state or fashion. He must not head mobs, or set the ton in dress. But I cannot call that situation nothing, which has the charge of all that is of the first importance to mankind, individually or collectively considered, temporally and eternally—which has the guardianship of religion and morals, and consequently of the manners which result from their influence." (92)

Mary remains unconvinced: "One does not see much of this influence and importance in society," she argues. And how can a clergyman be so influential when one "scarcely sees [him] out of his pulpit"?

Edmund tries to explain that preaching is not a clergyman's only business, and to enlarge on and explain his previous claim:

> "A fine preacher is followed and admired; but it is not in fine preaching only that a good clergyman will be useful in his parish and his neighbourhood, where the parish and neighbourhood are of a size capable of knowing his private character, and observing his general conduct.... And with regard to their influencing public manners, Miss Crawford must not misunderstand me, or suppose I mean to call [clergymen] the arbiters of good breeding, the regulators of refinement and courtesy, the masters of the ceremonies of life. The *manners* I speak of, might rather be called *conduct*, perhaps, the result of good principles; the effect, in short, of those doctrines which it is their duty to teach and recommend; and it will, I believe, be every where found, that as the clergy are, or are not what they ought to be, so are the rest of the nation."
> "Certainly," said Fanny with gentle earnestness.
> "There," cried Miss Crawford, "you have quite convinced Miss Price already." (93)

There is a touch of irony at Fanny's expense here. We see her as Mary sees her, as an insignificant good little thing; and she is still too much Edmund's creature, and his echo. Nevertheless, she is, with the reader, the spectator who sees more of the game than the contestants.

The dispute between Edmund and Mary is a fundamental one. It is the dispute between principle and style.[12] For her, as for her histrionic brother, who believes he would preach splendid sermons (341), preaching is all there is of a clergyman, because that is all that *appears*; it is the part of his profession that can be done with distinction and applause. But Edmund refuses to divorce status from function; he de-emphasizes the preaching, and insists on the practice: he is Jane Austen's version of Chaucer's poor parson. Edmund takes his stand on moral ground, Mary on aesthetic. So far they are distinguished in their general discussion on the duties and the status of clergymen.

However, the issue between them is personal and private too. In reply to Mary's gay, "There, you have quite convinced Miss Price already," Edmund urges,

> "I wish I could convince Miss Crawford too."
> "I do not think you ever will," said she with an arch smile; "I am just as much surprised now as I was at first that you should intend to take orders. You really are fit for something better. Come, do change your mind. It is not too late. Go into the law."

"Go into the law! with as much ease as I was told to go into this wilderness."

"Now you are going to say something about law being the worst wilderness of the two, but I forestall you; remember I have forestalled you." (93-4)

Mary maintains her gay and even frivolous tone, but there is more at issue here, as all three know, than a general dispute on the merits of various professions. Edmund's underlying argument might be translated thus: "Respect the calling I have chosen," he pleads, "because I want to marry you." Mary's underlying answer goes, "Well, I'm interested in your offer; but you must do something I think is worthy of *me*." They are neither of them fully conscious of this set of implications, but that is essentially the issue under discussion. That "Come, do change your mind. It is not too late," for all its playfulness, has its undertow of urgency.

In spite of Mary's trite witticism about law and the wilderness, Jane Austen evidently intends her readers to understand the wilderness emblematically. It was Mary who led the way into this wood, with its "serpentining" pathways, and Edmund enters it much as the Redcrosse Knight, accompanied by his Una, enters the Wandering Wood in which he encounters the female monster, Error. Related symbolism is unobtrusively developed elsewhere in the novel. Mary is the temptress, the siren, who plays the harp and sings. In another significant little scene involving the same trio, Edmund stands at the window with Fanny, who is like the figure of duty urging him to look up at the stars, while Mary goes to the piano to take part in a glee. He and Fanny agree to go out on the lawn to stargaze, but he finds himself unable to resist the music: "as it advanced, [Fanny] had the mortification of seeing him advance too, moving forward by gentle degrees towards the instrument, and when it ceased, he was close by the singers, among the most urgent in requesting to hear the glee again" (113). This Odysseus has neglected to have himself tied to the mast. Our last glimpse of Mary is to be of her attempt to lure Edmund back to her, with "a saucy playful smile," as he says, "seeming to invite, in order to subdue me" (459). But this time he is able to say Get thee behind me, Satan.[13]

To return to the Sotherton scene: after Mary's sally about the wilderness, Edmund admits he can never achieve a witticism, and "a general silence succeeded." Fanny, as she so often is, has been the most acute sufferer as the witness of this veiled courtship, and presently she indicates her pain:

"I wonder that I should be tired with only walking in this sweet wood; but the next time we come to a seat, if it is not disagreeable to you, I should be glad to sit down for a little while."

> "My dear Fanny," cried Edmund, immediately drawing her arm within his, "how thoughtless I have been! I hope you are not very tired. Perhaps," turning to Miss Crawford, "my other companion may do me the honour of taking an arm."
>
> "Thank you, but I am not at all tired." She took it, however, as she spoke, and the gratification of having her do so, of feeling such a connection for the first time, [here one might mark another hiatus //] made him a little forgetful of Fanny. "You scarcely touch me," said he. "You do not make me of any use. What a difference in the weight of a woman's arm from that of a man! At Oxford I have been a good deal used to have a man lean on me for the length of a street, and you are only a fly in the comparison." (94)

Now, that doesn't sound like D. H. Lawrence. Lawrence unkindly called Jane "old maid."[14] And she certainly doesn't expatiate on what he calls "That exquisite and immortal moment of a man's entry into the woman of his desire."[15] But nevertheless, Edmund registers, and within the bounds of polite converse, expresses the thrill he feels at this physical contact with Mary.

There is again an emblematic quality in this threesome—Edmund between his two women, the one needing his arm, the other consenting to take it temporarily. It is a recurring triangle. Later in the novel, Fanny is the chosen witness for another such scene: this one is literally a courtship, though played as a scene in a play. During the rehearsals for *Lovers' Vows*, first Mary and then Edmund separately seek out Fanny to hear their lines in the crucial proposal scene between Amelia and Anhalt. Fanny plays her role reluctantly enough:

> To prompt them must be enough for her; and it was sometimes *more* than enough; for she could not always pay attention to the book.... And agitated by the increasing spirit of Edmund's manner, had once closed the page and turned away exactly as he wanted help. It was imputed to very reasonable weariness, and she was thanked and pitied; but she deserved their pity, more than she hoped they would ever surmise. (170)

Fanny has been disliked by many because she has so much the air of a martyr; but her martyrdom is very real, for she is made to witness, and even to prompt, exchanges where the private signification is perfectly understandable and deeply painful to her.

Readers of *Mansfield Park* have often objected to what they take to be Jane Austen's summary treatment of the important matter of how Edmund, once he has lost Mary, comes to transfer his affections to Fanny:

> Scarcely had he done regretting Mary Crawford, and observing to Fanny how impossible it was that he should ever meet with such another woman, before it began to strike him whether a very different kind of woman

might not do just as well—or a great deal better.... I purposely abstain from dates on this occasion. (470)

But such readers have I think missed one of the major subsurface movements of the novel: Edmund's unconscious courtship of Fanny, which is concurrent with his deliberate courtship of Mary. The reader is constantly informed of how his love for Mary and his love for Fanny grow *together*. The three are always "in a cluster together" (86), they seem "naturally to unite" (90). The more Edmund's ardour kindles for Mary, the more fervent become his feelings for Fanny. He speaks of them as "the two dearest objects I have on earth" (264). When he confesses his love for Mary to Fanny, he calls *her* "Dearest Fanny!" and presses "her hand to his lips, with almost as much warmth as if it had been Miss Crawford's" (269). And when he writes to Fanny of his beloved, he tells her, "There is something soothing in the idea, that we have the same friend, and that whatever unhappy differences of opinion may exist between us, we are united in our love of you" (420). He has indeed needed Fanny's "prompting," even in his courtship of the other woman.

Of course the psychological probability of the confidante's becoming a principal in the love affair is frequently demonstrated in literature as in life. Ritualized comic versions of the situation appear several times in Shakespeare alone (not to mention *Lovers' Vows* itself), and Fanny in her role as prompter for Edmund might well say with Viola, "A barful strife! / Whoe'er I woo, myself would be his wife!" A more serious psychological study appears in *Henry Esmond*, where the hero woos Beatrix for a decade, making a confidante of her mother, and finally marries the mother instead. And George Eliot exploited the same situation for irony and pathos in the relation of Farebrother, Mary Garth and Fred Vincy, in *Middlemarch*.

Mary Crawford and Fanny, for Edmund, are a package deal; and at the end he simply discovers that he has mistaken the wrapping for the gift. So, in the scene at Sotherton I have been discussing, Edmund's decorous place between the two young ladies, courteously lending an arm to each, is an objective correlative for the passionate tensions of the eternal triangle.

The next scene I would like to mine is from *Persuasion*. It occurs during the walk to Winthrop, when Louisa Musgrove has just urged her sister Henrietta to visit her cousin and admirer Charles Hayter, in spite of the disapproval of the status-seeking Mary Musgrove, who feels she should connect herself better. Louisa boasts to Captain Wentworth of her part in the affair, while Anne accidentally overhears:

"And so, I made her go. I could not bear that she should be frightened from the visit by such nonsense. What!—would I be turned back from doing a thing that I had determined to do, and that I knew to be right, by the airs and interference of such a person?—or, of any person I may say. No,—I have no idea of being so easily persuaded. When I have made up my mind, I have made it. And Henrietta seemed entirely to have made up hers to call at Winthrop to-day—and yet, she was as near giving it up, out of nonsensical complaisance!"
"She would have turned back then, but for you?"
"She would indeed. I am almost ashamed to say it."
"Happy for her, to have such a mind as yours at hand!" (87)

Anyone with sense and discrimination can see that Louisa is expressing herself with more force than intelligence: the sister who urges a persuadable mind in one direction may be as blameworthy as the sister-in-law who urges it in the other. But, with the kind of deafness to nuance and delicacy that characterizes the Mrs. Eltons of the world, she insists on her own irreproachable rectitude. Louisa's strengths and deficiencies, however, are not so interesting to us as Wentworth's misjudgements of them. For him all discussions on the influence of one person over another relate to himself, and his broken engagement to Anne, and Lady Russell's persuasion that caused the breach. When he says, "Happy for her, to have such a mind as yours at hand!" he has mentally recast all the people in question, so that Henrietta has become Anne, himself Charles Hayter, Mary Lady Russell, and Louisa the advocate he wishes he himself had had eight years ago. The rights and wrongs of the case he has not yet come to terms with. All he feels now is, "*I* have suffered because Anne yielded to persuasion; therefore the others must have been wrong." This is the premise on which he bases his moral philosophy.

"Your sister is an amiable creature; but *yours* is the character of decision and firmness, I see. If you value her conduct or happiness, infuse as much of your own spirit into her, as you can. But this, no doubt, you have been always doing. It is the worst evil of too yielding and indecisive a character, that no influence over it can be depended on.—You are never sure of a good impression being durable. Every body may sway it." (88)

Here, of course, there is an irony for the reader. Wentworth is supposing that because Anne gave him up she is inconstant in her heart, whereas we know, as we listen with her, that *her* feelings have scarcely altered through eight years, and we will soon find out that the "firm" Louisa will transfer her affections in a few weeks.

"Let those who would be happy be firm [he continues].—Here is a nut," said he, catching one down from an upper bough. "To exemplify,—a beautiful glossy nut, which, blessed with original strength, has outlived all

> the storms of autumn. Not a puncture, not a weak spot any where.—This nut," he continued, with playful solemnity,—"While so many of its brethren have fallen and been trodden under foot, is still in possession of all the happiness that a hazel-nut can be supposed capable of." Then, returning to his former earnest tone: "My first wish for all, whom I am interested in, is that they should be firm. If Louisa Musgrove would be beautiful and happy in her November of life, she will cherish all her present powers of mind." (88)

His solemnity is not really playful, though he is conducting an entertaining conversation—speaking aphoristically, and illustrating his maxims by apt analogy with elements of the autumn landscape. If we did not know the circumstances, we would be forced to suppose that this man has a bee in his bonnet about firmness: he is almost obsessive. "My first wish for all, whom I am interested in, is that they should be firm"—a curious priority! And then, "If Louisa Musgrove would be beautiful and happy in her November of life, she will cherish all her present powers of mind." He is thinking of the contrast with Anne. Anne, as he resentfully thinks of her now, is not beautiful and happy, but faded and miserable, and so she deserves to be in this and every other November of her life. That is the feeling that underlies his analogy. And in his little parable of the nut he is wiser than he knows. Louisa, in comparison with Anne, does have a limited range of sensibility, and can perhaps hope to achieve not very much more than "all the happiness that a hazel-nut can be supposed capable of." We need hardly pause over the quality of his advice—thus encouraged by him, Louisa does "cherish all her present powers of mind," and, through her stubborn persistence on the Cobb at Lyme, nearly knocks out her brains altogether.

Captain Wentworth speaks with a weight of implication of which he is not, as Edmund is in the other scene, in control. His speech has been essentially an expression of his resentment against the persuadability of Anne Elliot, but the form it has taken is earnest praise of Louisa Musgrove.

> He had done,—and was unanswered. It would have surprised Anne, if Louisa could have readily answered such a speech—words of such interest, spoken with such serious warmth!—she could image what Louisa was feeling. For herself—[//] she feared to move, lest she should be seen. (88)

Captain Wentworth has essentially been saying: "Anne made me miserable by listening to someone else's advice"; Louisa has heard "What an admirable woman you are! I would like to make you happy." Anne has heard some combination of both. And from this time, particularly as Henrietta is now out of the picture, Captain Wentworth is considered by Anne and others to be virtually engaged to Louisa. He has committed himself to one woman because of her unlikeness to the one he is really thinking of.

From this commitment he is happily released by Louisa's fortunate facility in falling in love with Captain Benwick. He must then inform Anne that he had never been in love with Louisa. They are at a public assembly in Bath, and he must again make his declaration by indirection: "I regard Louisa Musgrove as a very amiable, sweet-tempered girl, and not deficient in understanding; but Benwick is something more" (182). *Now* he is in control of his language of implication, and Anne is perfectly able to translate it: "His opinion of Louisa Musgrove's inferiority, an opinion which he had seemed solicitous to give, his wonder at Captain Benwick... —all, all declared that he had a heart returning to her" (185). The full declaration—and it is fuller in this novel than in any of the six—is to come in a scene that exactly parallels the scene with the hazel-nut. Anne, in the fullness of her experience of eight years of fidelity to her love, speaks to Harville on the subject of constancy in men and women, while this time Wentworth is the eavesdropper. There is the same oblique communication between the two, and Wentworth like Anne has been put through the agony of jealousy. The spurious virtue of firmness has been re-categorized as obstinacy, and the real virtue of constancy is given due credit. As he listens, Wentworth is able to write, without indirection, words that are for Anne's eyes alone: "I am half agony, half hope.... I offer myself to you again with a heart even more your own, than when you almost broke it eight years and a half ago" (237). Anne had a smaller proportion of hope to agony in the previous scene, but she had the same feelings, though they were never voiced, there and through most of the novel.

Captain Wentworth is closer to being a Mr. Rochester than any other of Jane Austen's heroes. When Mr. Rochester finds himself tied to a woman he doesn't love, he "unlocked a trunk which contained a brace of loaded pistols" (*Jane Eyre*, Ch. 27), and when he is deserted by the one he does, "He grew savage—quite savage on his disappointment.... He got dangerous after he lost her. He would be alone, too" (Ch. 36). Now, perhaps Wentworth is not quite the stuff that Mr. Rochester is made of, and Jane Austen gives us no expanded account of his behaviour in his darkest hours after Anne rejected him. But we do have, in the course of conversation in the drawing-room at Uppercross, sufficient indication that he too has passed through the valley of the shadow. The Musgrove girls look for his first command, the Asp, in the navy list.

"You will not find her there, [he tells them]—Quite worn out and broken up. I was the last man who commanded her.—Hardly fit for service then.—Reported fit for home service for a year or two,—and so I was sent off to the West Indies."

The girls looked all amazement.

"The admiralty," he continued, "entertain themselves now and then, with sending a few hundred men to sea, in a ship not fit to be employed." (64-5)

And when his brother-in-law tells him he was lucky to get even such a command as the Asp, he admits, "I was as well satisfied with my appointment as you can desire. It was a great object with me, at that time, to be at sea,—a very great object. I wanted to be doing something" (65). The reference to his state of mind on being dismissed by Anne is clear. We have seen "no teare-floods, nor sigh-tempests," no pistols removed from the trunk, no withdrawal from the society of man—just a light-toned conversation with new acquaintance about the course of his profession. But Anne and the reader can understand that his mood was as close to being suicidal as Mr. Rochester's was, that he went to sea in a leaky ship, and would as soon have gone to the bottom as not. He has been Jane Austen's restrained version of Childe Harold, a "gloomy wanderer o'er the wave."

One more passage. Here is another neglected girl who looks on while the man she loves pursues an unworthy woman; but this time the point of view is centered not in the neglected girl, but in the unworthy one—in the erring Emma, in fact. To get the full emotional impact of all that is going on in this novel, we must sometimes make the imaginative leap that is needed to understand what the restrained Jane Fairfax is feeling, for Emma herself is of course hot-headed but cool-hearted, and for most of the novel doesn't know her own feelings.

Few of us can fail to have been impressed by the extraordinary power of the Box Hill scene. Its power resides in the fact that beneath all that conversation and badinage, and beneath the over-strained attempt to make a party go, there are two subsurface levels of action, which the alert reader is aware of, and which give the surface level particular intensity. On one level, at least one of the principals is not aware of what is going on: Emma's unconscious love for Mr. Knightley is beginning to force itself to the surface of her mind, and makes her realize that "she felt less happy than she had expected. She laughed because she was disappointed" (368). Frank Churchill suggests that for her entertainment everyone must reveal his thoughts; Mr. Knightley asks pointedly,

"Is Miss Woodhouse sure that she would like to hear what we are all thinking of?"

"Oh! no, no"—cried Emma, laughing as carelessly as she could—"Upon no account in the world." (369)

Divided from Mr. Knightley by the "principle of separation" that prevails (367), and pointlessly incurring his disapprobation by her joyless flirting with Frank Churchill, she is weighed down by a misery she can't define. From this state of mind arises her cruel joke at Miss Bates's expense, followed by her ride home in the carriage with the unconcealed tears running down her face.

In the other action, the principals are thoroughly awake to the language of implication, and are aiming covert barbs at each other which they mean to strike and wound. Frank Churchill and Jane Fairfax, the secret lovers, have quarrelled, and his pointed attentions to Emma are designed to express to Jane his independence of her. He is under *Miss Woodhouse*'s command; he implores *Miss Woodhouse* to choose and educate a wife for him, since he has no faith in his own choice. He and Jane proceed in their covert quarrel to break off their engagement. Frank says of the Eltons (who like himself and Jane met at a public watering-place) that they are "lucky" their marriage is as happy as it is. His apparently general comments are deeply insulting to Jane.

> "Very lucky—marrying as they did, upon an acquaintance formed only in a public place! . . .—for as to any real knowledge of a person's disposition that Bath, or any public place, can give—it is all nothing; there can be no knowledge. It is only by seeing women in their own homes, among their own set, just as they always are, that you can form any just judgment. Short of that, it is all guess and luck—and will generally be ill-luck. How many a man has committed himself on a short acquaintance, and rued it all the rest of his life!" (372)

Jane Fairfax has her cue to answer: "A hasty and imprudent attachment may arise—but there is generally time to recover from it afterwards" (373). "Jane," he can be understood to say—(I wish I could write the scene as Charlotte would have liked it; but then I like it the way it is)—"Jane, now that I've seen you in your sordid little home, with your dreary family, I'm thoroughly disillusioned, and I wish to God I hadn't got involved with you." "Frank," she may be supposed to reply, "get lost." At any rate, as Frank afterwards acknowledges, "She spoke her resentment in a form of words perfectly intelligible to me" (441).

That form of words is not, I suspect, perfectly intelligible to Charlotte Brontë and her allies. She accused Jane Austen of being deaf to the rhythms of the human heart, but she herself had no ear for the still small voice. She was attuned to what Scott called "The Big Bow-wow strain."[16]

In general terms I have been talking about the power of form to liberate rather than to limit. In art the restrictions of form and discipline do not confine, but rather *define*. "As well a well wrought urne becomes / The greatest ashes, as halfe-acre tombes"—the sentiment was shared and practised by Jane Austen, even if the metaphor would be hardly characteristic. Her novels are well wrought urns, where Charlotte Brontë's preference was more in the line of half-acre tombs. I have had occasion to quote Donne once before in this chapter; and, strange bedfellows as they seem at first sight, Donne and Jane Austen have much in common. They both have the conviction that it is not the quantity of experience that counts, but the quality; and they both have the concomitant power to make "one little roome, an every where." They find the world's room in a bed, in a relationship, or in Highbury, or in those "3 or 4 Families in a Country Village" that Jane Austen delighted in writing about (*Letters*, 401).

We all know that Jane Austen was an ironist. Studies of her irony have formed the mainstay of much recent criticism of her novels. But we usually associate irony with the intellect: we think of it as a polemical tool, or as a means of creating comedy through its illumination of incongruity; we assume that the ironist maintains a cerebral detachment, like Mr. Bennet's in *Pride and Prejudice*. Marvin Mudrick even heads one of the chapters of his book on Jane Austen's irony "Irony and Convention *versus* Feeling."[17] But irony and feeling are not necessarily opposed: there is an irony used to express emotion as well as an irony used to make fun of it. Arthur Sidgewick pointed this out in an early and illuminating article on the term: "It often comes about," he said, "that while the lower stages of feeling can be expressed, the higher stages must be suggested. In the ascent the full truth will do; but the climax can only be reached by irony."[18] I do not claim quite this much for Jane Austen—she does not deal in the tragic experience of an Oedipus or an Othello; but her power of understatement, and ability to express feelings by indirection, inform her novels with emotional intensity. She offers us far more than the *surface* of the lives of genteel English people.

CHAPTER III

Love and Pedagogy[1]

"Your lessons found the weakest part," Vanessa complained to her tutor Cadenus, "Aim'd at the head, and reach'd the heart." Swift and Vanessa weren't the first couple, nor yet the last, to discover that the master-pupil relationship can be a highly aphrodisiac one.[2] From Heloise and Abelard to Eliza Doolittle and Henry Higgins, history and literature produce recurrent examples of relations that evolve from the academic to the erotic. And Jane Austen's novels afford in themselves a range of possibilities in the operations of teaching and learning as an emotional bond. As Lionel Trilling points out, Jane Austen "was committed to the ideal of 'intelligent love', according to which the deepest and truest relationship that can exist between human beings is pedagogic. This relationship consists in the giving and receiving of knowledge about right conduct, in the formation of one person's character by another, the acceptance of another's guidance in one's own growth."[3]

Jane Austen, in exploring this subject so thoroughly, perhaps sets a standard for the nineteenth-century novel, which continued, partly because of its strongly didactic intention, to present love stories in which the heroine falls in love with a man who is her tutor, or her mentor, or her superior in age, experience or authority. No doubt there is an Oedipal element in the relationship: the daughter is sexually attracted to the embodiment of her father's loving rule.[4] But society generally condones and even encourages this attitude, where it usually looks with disapproval or disgust on the young man who marries the older woman, however wise she may be.

Charlotte Brontë, in spite of her scorn of Jane Austen for knowing nothing of the Passions, nonetheless fastened on the same central relationship for her most passionate attachments. Mr. Rochester is "the master," and Jane, equal soul though she is, looks up to him from the stance of servant, daughter, pupil:[5] "I love Thornfield," she acknowledges; "I love it, because I have lived in it a full and delightful life.... I have talked, face to face, with what I reverence; with what I delight in,—with an original, a vigorous, an expanded mind. I have known you, Mr. Rochester" (*Jane Eyre*, ch. 23). Lucy Snowe's relation to Monsieur Paul is literally pedagogic, since he becomes her tutor: "His mind was indeed my library, and whenever it was opened to me, I entered bliss" (*Villette*, Ch. 33). Charlotte Brontë, pupil of Monsieur Héger, knew what it was like to be in love with the master, and in her novels she charges the pedagogic relationships with a passion which, though she apparently did not notice it in Jane Austen's novels, she might well have found there in a refined but still intense form.

George Eliot too examined how "potent in us is the infused action of another soul, before which we bow in complete love" (*Daniel Deronda*, ch. 65); but her treatment of the pedagogic relationship differs from Charlotte Brontë's in that it introduces an element of grim irony. Perhaps she remembered with some qualms of embarrassment her adolescent susceptibility to handsome language teachers and elderly pedants,[6] and sought to exorcise the memories. Maggie Tulliver begs Philip Wakem, "Teach me everything —wouldn't you? Greek and everything?" (*The Mill on the Floss*, II, ch. 6), and he does undertake to develop her and direct her reading, falling deeply in love with her in the process; but her love for him is a thin cerebral quantity that cannot match the force of her strong sexual attraction to Stephen Guest. Dorothea Brooke looks joyfully forward to a marriage in which "she would be allowed to live continually in the light of a mind that she could reverence," but finds that Mr. Casaubon's mind is only a series of dark "vaults where he walked taper in hand" (*Middlemarch*, I, Chs. 5, 10). And Gwendolen Harleth, eager to receive Deronda's instruction and render herself in return, discovers that though he is ready enough with instruction, he doesn't want *her*.

Henry James goes further still in exploring the sinister implications in the pedagogic relationship. That it fascinated him is testified by his first novel, *Watch and Ward*, which is about a man who brings up his ward, educates her, and marries her at last. But he leads us through a series of disturbing speculations about the right of one mind to govern another, in presenting Maisie, who is used for dubious purposes in the sexual relations of her parents and parent surrogates; Miles and Flora, who apparently either pervert or are perverted by their governess; and Isabel Archer, who negates herself by trying to conform to the aesthetic standards of the manipulators who surround her. The culmination is the horrible premise of the narrator of *The Sacred Fount*, that what one gives—of youth, of wisdom, of joy—is by definition no longer one's own: that the donor becomes, in the process of giving, correspondingly depleted. You can't eat your cake and have it too. When he hears of how much grace and intelligence a certain lady has imparted to a man, he asks incredulously, "She keeps her wit then, ... in spite of all she pumps into others?" (Ch. 1). And he gradually persuades his interlocutor,

"Whoever she is, she gives all she has. She keeps nothing back—nothing for herself."

"I see—because *he* takes everything. He just cleans her out." (Ch. 3)

Similar metaphors are multiplied, until the one who gives is seen as a "victim," the one who receives as "the author of the sacrifice," and we are presented with a complete theory of human relations as a system of parasitism, of society as composed of vampires and victims. The narrator of *The Sacred Fount* may be a crazy hypothesizer, but James gives his theory a certain authority when he returns to the giving and taking relationship again in *The Ambassadors*, where it is hard to resist the conclusion that Chad Newsome has grown fat and sleek while Madame de Vionnet has dwindled to a diaphanous wraith.

Such a progression suggests why Lionel Trilling notes that "the idea of a love based in pedagogy may seem quaint to some modern readers and repellent to others." But he goes on—"unquestionably it plays a decisive part in the power and charm of Jane Austen's art."[7] What to James is suspect and potentially horrible, for Jane Austen is a source of power and charm. For her the pedagogic relationship is not parasitic but symbiotic, a relationship that is mutual and joyful: it blesseth him that gives, and him that takes. The happy resolutions of her novels celebrate the achieved integration of head and heart that is represented by the pupil and teacher coming to loving accord. Novelists of more tragic vision are unable to visualise so complete a reconcilement. A recurring pattern in the novels of the Brontës, George Eliot, Hardy, Lawrence and others shows a split between the intellectual and the passionate, the Apollonian and the Dionysian, the spiritual and the physical; and the task of the central character is to choose *between* alternatives—between Edgar Linton and Heathcliff, St. John Rivers and Mr. Rochester, Philip Wakem and Stephen Guest, Angel Clare and Alec D'Urberville, Hermione Roddice and Ursula Brangwen. The final choice may be too difficult, and Cathy, Maggie and Tess are destroyed in the process of making it; but even where the choice is made and a fortunate resolution achieved, some loss is implied in the rejected alternative.

The alternative men for the Austen heroine—Wickham, Crawford, Churchill *et al.*—are far from presenting the same agonising choice of alternatives. Her feelings for them—if aroused at all, which is doubtful—are transitory and swiftly recognized as a delusion. She generally recognizes joyfully that "We needs must love the highest when we see it, / Not Lancelot, nor another"—and without having to go through the extent of Guinevere's pain and error in the process. The union of Fanny Price with Edmund, say, is entire and satisfying—because Edmund has not only "formed her mind" but also "gained her affections" (*MP*, 64), and at the same time.

Richard Simpson, in his fine early study of Jane Austen, pointed out her commitment to "the Platonic idea that the giving and receiving of knowledge . . . is the truest and strongest foundation of love." But he goes on to suggest that this love between her heroes and heroines doesn't amount to much: "Friendship, to judge from her novels, was enough for her; she did not want to exaggerate it into passionate love."[8] Strongly as he is convinced of her merits, he seems to agree with Charlotte Brontë that the stormy sisterhood of the passions have no place in her work, and that she opts for esteem rather than passion as the basis of a successful marriage. But Jane Austen will not accept that division—for her the full and mutual engagement of head and heart is what *is* passionate; and any substitute, like Marianne's love for Willoughby, is not only founded on a delusion, but a delusion in itself.

The pattern, however, is of course far more varied than this simplification suggests. Ian Watt comments, "As has often been observed, [Jane Austen's] young heroines finally marry older men—comprehensive epitomes of the Augustan norms such as Mr. Darcy and Mr. Knightley. Her novels in fact dramatise the process whereby feminine and adolescent values are painfully educated in the norms of the mature, rational and educated male world."[9] I don't think one needs to be a woman to recognize that as a dangerous generalization. Elizabeth teaches Darcy as much as he teaches her; Anne and Fanny, in the main course of the novels' action, remain morally static while Wentworth and Edmund get the painful education; and Marianne, though she certainly has plenty to learn, learns from her sister. That leaves Catherine and Emma, who do get educated in the norms of their men; but even they have a certain power whereby their Pygmalions find that Galatea has turned the tables on them.

Characteristically enough, Jane Austen starts out by being ironic, even satiric, on the theme that she continues to develop through the whole body of her novels. In walking with the Tilneys, Catherine Morland discovers her ignorance on the subject of landscape and the picturesque:

> She was heartily ashamed of her ignorance. A misplaced shame. Where people wish to attach, they should always be ignorant. To come with a well-informed mind, is to come with an inability of administering to the vanity of others, which a sensible person would always wish to avoid. A woman especially, if she have the misfortune of knowing any thing, should conceal it as well as she can. (*NA*, 110-111)

And the narrator proceeds with an aphoristic discussion of how, though some men will be content with mere ignorance in a woman, most will be satisfied with nothing less than imbecility. Such satire leaves Catherine comparatively unscathed; it is Tilney who needs his vanity administering to.

The satire on the pedagogic relation notwithstanding, Jane Austen goes on to study its operation in realistic terms, and sympathetically:

> In the present instance, she confessed and lamented her want of knowledge; ... and a lecture on the picturesque immediately followed, in which his instructions were so clear that she soon began to see beauty in every thing admired by him, and her attention was so earnest, that he became perfectly satisfied of her having a great deal of natural taste. (111)

He sounds like Emma concluding of Harriet that she is "so pleasantly grateful for being admitted to Hartfield, and so artlessly impressed by the appearance of every thing in so superior a style to what she had been used to, that she must have good sense and deserve encouragement" (*E*, 23). Jane Austen was perfectly aware of the element of self-love in the pedagogic relationship, as was Swift:

> What he had planted, now was grown;
> His Virtues she might call her own ...
> Self-love, in Nature rooted fast,
> Attends us first, and leaves us last:
> Why she likes him, admire not at her,
> She loves her self, and that's the matter.   ("Cadenus and Vanessa")

Tilney is a kind of god to Catherine—"It was no effort to Catherine to believe that Henry Tilney could never be wrong" (114): but the creature has a concomitant power over her creator, as we find in numbers of such incidents as his dance with her, during which she "enjoyed her usual happiness with Henry Tilney, listening with sparkling eyes to every thing he said; and, in finding him irresistible, becoming so herself" (131). Tilney may well find that "a teachableness of disposition in a young lady is a great blessing" (174).

And, unlike Emma with Harriet, he does have much to teach her, and she duly benefits from his instruction. His insistence on precision with language, as Stuart Tave suggests,[10] teaches her not only to have the right word by which to express herself, but also to define and refine the sentiment that is to be expressed. Like Henry Higgins, to some extent he creates a new identity for her by giving her a new language. And if novel readers are disposed to be disappointed, as Jane Austen predicted, "that his affection originated in nothing better than gratitude" (243), that he loves her only because she has made it so plain that she loves him, we may be consoled to reflect that Tilney needs Catherine—though of course not as much as she needs him. She can't lecture him or consciously re-form him; but she can recognize that "he indulged himself a little too much with the foibles of others" (29)—an indulgence we later see more dangerously practised by Mr. Bennet. And in fact Tilney is not much to be admired in drawing out the absurdities of Mrs. Allen. However just his ridicule of affectation, however minute his discriminations, he is occasionally on the verge of becoming a rather glib satirist, what Isabella Thorpe would call a "quiz." He is captivated by Catherine's fresh responses and quickly engaged feelings—so that when, like Miranda looking on the brave new world, she exclaims, "Oh! who can ever be tired of Bath?" he answers with genuine appreciation, "Not those who bring such fresh feelings of every sort to it, as you do." (79). Charmingly disenchanted as he is, he needs those fresh feelings, and responds to them.

Nevertheless, we are not again to find in Jane Austen's novels so apt and so docile a pupil as Catherine Morland. To move from *Northanger Abbey* to *Pride and Prejudice* is like turning from *The Taming of the Shrew* to *Much Ado*. Henry Tilney and Petruchio have it all, or nearly all, their own way, and have comparatively little to learn from their two Catherines; but between Elizabeth and Darcy, as between Beatrice and Benedick, matters are more evenly balanced. They are both student-teachers; not that either deliberately sets out to instruct or to learn from the other—but they do very resoundingly teach each other a lesson. And, again as with Beatrice and Benedick, the state that exists between them is war: "They never meet but there's a skirmish of wit between them" (*Much Ado About Nothing*, I, i).

The similarity between these two gayest of their authors' works sometimes tempts me to speculate whether Jane Austen was consciously following Shakespeare's play.[11] Beatrice, "born in a merry hour" (II, i) is surely kin to Elizabeth, who "dearly love[s] a laugh" (*PP*, 57), and her comment, "I was born to speak all mirth and no matter" (II, i), seems echoed in Jane Austen's playful assertion that her novel was "rather too light, and bright, and sparkling; ... it wants to be stretched out here and there with a long chapter of sense, if it could be had" (*Letters*, 299).

The analogy is pertinent not only for suggesting the exuberant quality of both works, but for illuminating the sexual piquancy of the love-war relation, that gives such delightful force and suggestiveness to works like *The Rape of the Lock, Pamela, Jane Eyre*, and the wife of Bath's prologue and tale. I find it hard to credit that anyone who has read *Pride and Prejudice* could subscribe to the view of Miss Austen as an old maid who wrote sexless novels—this novel to my ear fairly rings with the jubilant fertility of spring.[12] Elizabeth's physical vitality, expressing itself in her running, her "jumping over stiles and springing over puddles" (32), and so on, is a sexual vitality too; and Darcy's strongly sexual response to her, as he gradually and unwillingly succumbs to her "fine eyes," is quite sufficiently dramatized. We see in Elizabeth as in Beatrice the subsumed attraction that is behind their antagonism—although they always fight with their men, they are always thinking of them. Beatrice, separated as she thinks from Benedick in the masked dance, says almost wistfully, "I would he had boarded me"; and Elizabeth can't see Miss de Bourgh without reflecting, "She looks sickly and cross.—Yes, she will do for him very well"—the "him" in her consciousness being Darcy (158). But relations between her and Darcy proceed stormily: she refuses to dance with him, and he is the more attracted. When she does dance with him, she quarrels with him about Wickham. They spar in the dance, skirmish at the piano, fence in conversation. Beatrice's sallies on "Signior Mountanto" are echoed in Elizabeth's witticisms at Darcy's expense: "I am perfectly convinced...that Mr. Darcy has no defect. He owns it himself without disguise" (57). Such is their "merry war"—very provocative, very delightful.

But the battles are not love play only—they have their serious issues, in which, without usually intending it, the antagonists set up their standards for the other to conform to or reject. Elizabeth is initially closest to being the pedagogue. Bingley recognizes her as "a studier of character" (42); and in admitting, "Follies and nonsense, whims and inconsistencies *do* divert me, I own, and I laugh at them whenever I can" (57), she achieves the status of a kind of licensed satirist during her brief stay at Netherfield. She makes full use of that licence in her critical analyses of character. In a playful context, she is a teacher catechising a potential student in order to place him:

> "Follies and nonsense,...I suppose, are precisely what you are without."
> "Perhaps that is not possible for anyone [replies Darcy]. But it has been the study of my life to avoid those weaknesses which often expose a strong understanding to ridicule."
> "Such as vanity and pride."
> "Yes, vanity is a weakness indeed. But pride—where there is a real superiority of mind, pride will be always under good regulation."
> Elizabeth turned away to hide a smile.
> "Your examination of Mr. Darcy is over, I presume," said Miss Bingley; —"and pray what is the result?" (57)

"The study of my life," "real superiority of mind," "good regulation," "examination"—this is classroom terminology. And though Darcy goes through this play catechism with the smiling detachment of an adult who has already done with exams, he is to recall and eventually be changed by Elizabeth's standards as implied in these dialogues.

There are three main subjects on which Elizabeth "examines" him in the course of the novel, and in which he acquits himself with varying degrees of credit, at various attempts.

The first issue is his right of influence over Bingley, canvassed at length, in a Netherfield discussion complete with a hypothetical case, as in an exam question (48-51). Ironically Elizabeth, who is far from being an infallible teacher, takes the opposite side in this argument from that she is to take in practice afterwards—here she defends Bingley's "merit" in his readiness "to yield readily—easily—to the *persuasion* of a friend" (50), whereas later she is to be indignant that Darcy makes him do just that.

The second aspect of Darcy's character that Elizabeth probes at Netherfield is what she calls, when he admits, "my good opinion once lost is lost for ever," his "implacable resentment" (58). Here the practical test Elizabeth administers is Wickham, against whom she believes that that resentment has been unjustly vented. Unjustifiable influence over his friend, and brutal persecution of his enemy: these are the two offences she accuses Darcy of in the first proposal scene. She has examined him as a candidate for her hand, and she fails him resoundingly. Having failed the *viva*, Darcy voluntarily sits a written exam—his letter—not to qualify himself for the same position, but to justify himself as a man of right conduct. This paper is enough to teach the teacher how wrong she has been, how "blind, partial, prejudiced, absurd."

> "How despicably have I acted!" she cried.—"I, who have prided myself on my discernment!—I, who have valued myself on my abilities! ... I have courted prepossession and ignorance, and driven reason away, where either were concerned. Till this moment, I never knew myself." (208)

It is a salutary lesson for one who has been more fond of detecting shortcomings in others than in herself.

Darcy is to be further exonerated from the charge of implacable resentment by his remarkably forbearing behaviour to Elizabeth herself, who certainly gives provocation for resentment: after she quarrels with him in the dance, his feelings for her "soon procured her pardon" (94); and though his letter after her insulting refusal begins in bitterness, "the adieu is charity itself" (368). He has been tested by having had a lot to put up with; and he has been admirably tolerant and forgiving.

However, on the third issue Darcy has more to learn, and does not acquit himself creditably until the last part of the novel. It is not a question of conduct or principle, but of manners. Again the matter is playfully canvassed between them in conversation—as usual, with an audience at hand—this time at the piano at Rosings. Elizabeth threatens to tell Colonel Fitzwilliam of Darcy's misdemeanours in Hertfordshire:

> "You shall hear then—but prepare yourself for something very dreadful. The first time of my ever seeing him in Hertfordshire, you must know, was at a ball—and at this ball, what do you think he did? He danced only four dances! I am sorry to pain you—but so it was. He danced only four dances, though gentlemen were scarce; and, to my certain knowledge, more than one young lady was sitting down in want of a partner. Mr. Darcy, you cannot deny the fact." ...
>
> "I certainly have not the talent which some people possess," said Darcy, "of conversing easily with those I have never seen before. I cannot catch their tone of conversation, or appear interested in their concerns, as I often see done."
>
> "My fingers," said Elizabeth, "do not move over this instrument in the masterly manner which I see so many women's do. They have not the same force or rapidity, and do not produce the same expression. But then I have always supposed it to be my own fault—because I would not take the trouble of practising. It is not that I do not believe *my* fingers as capable as any other woman's of superior execution." (175)

Elizabeth's shortcomings as a pedagogue are still apparent in the continuing operation of that initial incident at the Meryton assembly that wounded her vanity, but here in essence she is right. Her analogy is apt—she lets Darcy know that gracious manners are not acquired simply as a ready-made gift from heaven, but that they are a skill, to be developed like other skills by exertion and practice. But Darcy, though he accepts her analogy, misapplies it and so doesn't profit from her instruction: "You are perfectly right," he acknowledges, "... No one admitted to the privilege of hearing you, can think any thing wanting. We neither of us perform to strangers" (176). But piano-playing is an accomplishment that anyone may choose or not choose to develop; gracious manners are a duty that everyone must practise, and most particularly those with Darcy's prominent position in the world. Again, it takes a practical issue to make the point. Darcy's churlish first proposal brings a fierce rebuke which this time sinks in, so that he can even quote it months afterwards: "Your reproof, so well applied, I shall never forget: 'had you behaved in a more gentleman-like manner.' Those were your words" (367). In the interval, like a good pupil, he has made a conscious effort "to correct my temper," and he displays his newly acquired skill when they meet at Pemberley:

"My object *then*," replied Darcy, "was to shew you, by every civility in my power, that I was not so mean as to resent the past; and I hoped to obtain your forgiveness, to lessen your ill opinion, by letting you see that your reproofs had been attended to." (370)

In this matter he has acknowledged his shortcomings and studied to correct them; and he has been an apt scholar: "You taught me a lesson," he acknowledges fervently (369). Like Benedick, he has resolved, "I must not seem proud. Happy are they that hear their detractions and can put them to mending" (II, iii).

Elizabeth has had plenty to learn too, but Darcy, though he is the occasion of her increased self-knowledge, is not so clearly the agent. The theoretical discussions at Netherfield and Rosings, which are subsequently so neatly put to the test, are about Darcy's behaviour, not Elizabeth's. Hers have been the faults of the examiner who has overestimated her qualifications and totally misjudged her examinees. They are faults not of conduct but of judgement; so that in the process whereby her failing candidate proves himself eminently qualified, and her favoured student does the reverse, she has come to know her shortcomings and herself.

On the question of Wickham's wrongs and Darcy's supposedly implacable resentment, she was entirely misguided, and Darcy had no fault to correct; and on the first issue canvassed between them, his influence on Bingley, she has learned that it is wrong only if exerted in the wrong direction; she ceases to be fanatical in her views here, but it is an issue that will arise again for playful debate between them. Darcy does still unblushingly keep Bingley under strict if friendly surveillance, and Bingley dares propose to Jane only with Darcy's permission:

> Elizabeth longed to observe that Mr. Bingley had been a most delightful friend; so easily guided that his worth was invaluable; but she checked herself. She remembered that he had yet to learn to be laught at, and it was rather too early to begin. (371)

That is a charming little preview of their marriage, confirming Elizabeth's conviction that "It was an union that must have been to the advantage of both" (312). Elizabeth, by the time they are engaged, has learned some tact and forbearance in the exercise of her wit; and Darcy, having learned manners, must go on learning—he must learn to be laughed at.

In *Pride and Prejudice* we see the pedagogic relationship stormily in process; in *Mansfield Park* it is virtually a *fait accompli* by the time the main action of the novel begins. By the end of the second chapter we get a summary of Edmund's central role in Fanny's education, and her response:

> His attentions were ... of the highest importance in assisting the improvement of her mind, and extending its pleasures. He knew her to be clever, to have a quick apprehension as well as good sense. ... He recommended the books which charmed her leisure hours, he encouraged her taste, and corrected her judgment. ... In return for such services she loved him better than any body in the world except William; her heart was divided between the two. (22)

By his early pedagogic role he has "formed her mind and gained her affections" (64). That state of affairs is memorably dramatized in the stargazing scene, where Fanny seeks to hold Edmund's attention by rhapsodizing over the natural beauty he has taught her to admire. "Here's harmony!" she exclaims, "Here's repose ... "

> "I like to hear your enthusiasm, Fanny. It is a lovely night, and they are much to be pitied who have not been taught to feel in some degree as you do—who have not at least been given a taste for nature in early life. They lose a great deal."
> "*You* taught me to think and feel on the subject, cousin."
> "I had a very apt scholar." (113)

At this point, however, Edmund is disposed to turn from his faithful creature to metal more attractive. Fanny's story is to begin when, as the now qualified star pupil, she watches her honoured master stray into error and pain,—led there by her rival the wayward pupil. What she has learned is put to its severest test when she must detach the learning from the tutor, and subject him to the tests of the very principles he has taught her.

It is noteworthy that "the first actual pain" that Mary Crawford occasions Fanny is caused when Edmund adopts the pedagogic stance with her —he teaches her to ride. His instructions to Fanny have always had a strongly moral cast: "You are sorry to leave Mamma, my dear little Fanny," he once comforted her, "which shows you to be a very good girl" (15)—and to maintain that role of the good girl in Edmund's estimation becomes her constant practice. But to Mary Crawford, whose attractions are more overtly physical, he initially teaches a physical activity. When Fanny, neglected and sorry for herself, watches from afar, she has cause to feel a pang at the physical intimacy that his instruction promotes:

> After a few minutes, they stopt entirely, Edmund was close to her, he was speaking to her, he was evidently directing her management of the bridle, he had hold of her hand; she saw it, or the imagination supplied what the eye could not reach. (67)

Fanny as a child had her own feelings warmed by such attentions from Edmund, when he ruled her lines for her letters, and stood by "to assist her with his penknife or his orthography, as either were wanted" (16). Now she is naturally quick to discover Edmund's attraction to his new pupil; and he is soon making her his confidante in his discussion of the shortcomings and charms of her rival.

> "I am glad you saw it all as I did" [he tells her after one such discussion].
> Having formed her mind and gained her affections, he had a good chance of her thinking like him; though at this period, and on this subject, there began now to be some danger of dissimilarity, for he was in a line of admiration of Miss Crawford, which might lead him where Fanny could not follow. (64)

It is in this direction that Fanny's story is to develop. She has been and is a good pupil, and the love that grew out of the pedagogic relation is to remain constant; but Fanny is to graduate from the status of pupil to adult in the process of separating her judgement from Edmund's, and detecting him in error. Fanny as pupil "regarded her cousin as an example of every thing good and great.... Her sentiments towards him were compounded of all that was respectful, grateful, confiding, and tender" (37). Fanny as adolescent wonders, "Could it be possible? Edmund so inconsistent.... Was he not wrong?" (156). Fanny as adult discovers, "He is blinded, and nothing will open his eyes" (424). But the pupil is morally debarred from opening his master's eyes, even though he recognizes her sound judgement and even reverses their roles by applying to her for advice: she cannot in honour denigrate her rival; hence her story must be a "trial," like Pamela's; and like Jane Austen's other actively passive heroines, Elinor and Anne, she must achieve through endurance rather than through action.

Mary Crawford, though she outclasses Fanny as a horsewoman, proves to be morally a totally intractable pupil. Edmund's most sustained effort in instructing her, as we have seen, is the conversation in the wood at Sotherton, where he carefully justifies his decision to enter the ministry, and persuasively explains the importance of a clergyman's duties. His lecture elicits an earnest "Certainly" from Fanny, but Mary Crawford asserts, "I am just as much surprised now as I was at first that you should intend to take orders" (93). She is simply determined not to listen: her mind is closed. And her very recalcitrance has its attractions for the teacher, who begins to succumb to that danger, not unknown to many of us, of paying most attention to the worst students: "He still reasoned with her, but in vain. She would not calculate, she would not compare. She would only smile and assert. The greatest degree of rational consistency could not have been more engaging, and they talked with mutual satisfaction" (96). And—again a familiar fault in pedagogues—he excuses her shortcomings as a moral student by blaming her previous educators: "Yes, that uncle and aunt! They have injured the finest mind!" (269).

Though Mary closes her mind to Edmund's influence, she is ambitious to influence *him*. And in her case it is not that her chief end is his moral welfare, but that she enjoys power. When she urges him to go into law she could conceivably have his good, as well as her own, in view; but in the matter of the play her tactics in persuading him to take the part of Anhalt are directed not only to getting him to play opposite her, but also simply to conquering him, because she relishes the triumph of making him act against his principles. Her fondest memory is of this victory: "His sturdy spirit to bend as it did! Oh, it was sweet beyond expression" (358). This sinister bit of gloating is another of the touches that remind us of Mary as temptress, seductress—as even Satanic.

Lovers' Vows provides a paradigm for the novel in that Edmund's role is Anhalt, who is literally the tutor of the heroine, Amelia. There are some crude statements there of themes Jane Austen enlarges on more subtly in the novel. Amelia tells her tutor, for instance, "My father has more than once told me that he who forms my mind I should always consider as my greatest benefactor. [*looking down*] And my heart tells me the same" (503-4).[13] And when Anhalt admits that "love" is the subject of their discourse, Amelia pursues, "[*going up to him*]. Come, then, teach it me—teach it me as you taught me geography, languages, and other important things" (506). Such might well be Fanny's sentiments, though of course she would never voice them. But it is Mary who plays Amelia's part: Mary has Amelia's brass, and Amelia's sense that her tutor is her social inferior—a sense that ultimately makes her unable to accept Edmund. But Fanny has been the docile and loving pupil. Amelia's role of the enamoured pupil combines Edmund's two women.

Emma, like Mary Crawford, is a bad pupil. They both have the talents to be good students, but the temperament to resist instruction. But though that is the whole of Mary's story, it is only a part of Emma's.

The novel opens on the evening of Miss Taylor's withdrawal from Hartfield, and Mr. Knightley's consequent friendly visit. Miss Taylor, we hear at the outset, has long been Emma's friend rather than her governess, and Emma, though "highly esteeming Miss Taylor's judgment," has been "directed chiefly by her own" (*E*, 5). Mr. Knightley is to tell Miss Taylor affectionately that she is "very fit for a wife, but not at all for a governess" (38). Still, she has been there, and now she has gone. That scene introduces not only the marriage theme of the novel, and "the question of dependence or independence"[14] but also the theme of Emma's education. Exit governess, enter governor: "Mr. Knightley, in fact, was one of the few people who could see faults in Emma Woodhouse, and the only one who ever told her of them: ... this was not particularly agreeable to Emma herself" (11). That is the initial situation, which we see dramatized at length in subsequent scenes. Emma doesn't like to be told she has anything to learn, and she argues.

On nearly all the questions at issue between them—and the working out of these constitutes the novel's structure—Mr. Knightley is right and Emma is wrong. Mr. Knightley condemns her matchmaking propensity: "Your time has been properly and delicately spent," he says with sarcasm, "if you have been endeavouring for the last four years to bring about this marriage" (12). But Emma insists, "Only one more [match] ... ; only for Mr. Elton"(13). And at the end she realizes how "with unpardonable arrogance [she had] proposed to arrange everybody's destiny" (413). Mr. Knightley objects to Emma's intimacy with Harriet, whom he calls "the very worst sort of companion that Emma could possibly have" (38). Emma maintains the intimacy notwithstanding, but is to exclaim at last, "Oh God! that I had never seen her!" (411). Mr. Knightley wants her to recognize Jane Fairfax's better claims to attention, but Emma persists in neglecting her, until she is made aware of her "past injustice towards Miss Fairfax" (421). Mr. Knightley tells her she is not sufficiently considerate towards Miss Bates, but his hints are not "equal to counteract the persuasion of its being very disagreeable" (155); until she eventually reproaches herself bitterly, "How could she have been so brutal, so cruel to Miss Bates!" (376). The only matter on which Mr. Knightley's judgement is not fully to be trusted is the merits, or lack of them, of Frank Churchill, and here Emma is shrewd:

> "You seem determined to think ill of him."
> "Me!—not at all," replied Mr. Knightley, rather displeased. (149)

His jealousy, quite forgivably, is the only passion that will lead his otherwise sound judgement astray.

So, as in *Pride and Prejudice*, there is the beautifully symmetrical pattern of the precept laid down and discussed in theory, the practical test, and the access of knowledge with experience. Emma is the wayward pupil; she does not simply close her mind like Mary Crawford, but she refuses to acknowledge she has anything to learn for as long as she can. And there is a focus of emotional intensity in their arguments—in Mr. Knightley's pleasure when Emma seems to have taken his advice, his disappointment when she turns out to be unreformed; in Emma's fluctuations of rebelliousness and fear of him in his "tall indignation" (60), and her schemes for placating him without actually taking his advice. In the scene where he exclaims, "Nonsense, errant nonsense, as ever was talked!" to her argument that Robert Martin is not fit for Harriet,

> Emma made no answer, and tried to look cheerfully unconcerned, but was really feeling uncomfortable and wanting him very much to be gone. She did not repent what she had done; she still thought herself a better judge of such a point of female right and refinement than he could be; but yet she had a sort of habitual respect for his judgment in general, which made her dislike having it so loudly against her; and to have him sitting just opposite to her in angry state, was very disagreeable. (65)

She cares about his disapproval, "she was sorry, but could not repent" (69). Like other wayward pupils who would rather resort to wiles than learn the lesson, she contrives a reconciliation with him while they are in physical contact, dandling their niece. "It did assist; for though he began with grave looks and short questions, he was soon led on to ... take the child out of her arms with all the unceremoniousness of perfect amity" (98).

On another occasion she plays with his eagerness for her properly appreciating Jane Fairfax. He warmly praises her attentions as hostess; "I am happy you approved," she says, smiling; but deliberately adds her old objection, "Miss Fairfax is reserved" (170-1).

> "My dear Emma," said he, moving from his chair into one close by her, "you are not going to tell me, I hope, that you had not a pleasant evening."
> "Oh! no; I was pleased with my own perseverance in asking questions, and amused to think how little information I obtained."
> "I am disappointed," was his only answer....
> Emma saw his anxiety, and wishing to appease it, at least for the present, said, and with a sincerity which no one could question—
> "She is a sort of elegant creature that one cannot keep one's eyes from. I am always watching her to admire; and I do pity her from my heart."
> Mr. Knightley looked as if he were more gratified than he cared to express. (171)

Here we trace the emotions of the pedagogue, eager for his student's progress: his warm physical approach, his distress in her backsliding, his gratification in the appeasement.

Emma as rebellious student often tries to bring Mr. Knightley round to her way of thinking, and occasionally has the pedagogue's pleasure in success. When he acknowledges Harriet's claims by dancing with her after Mr. Elton's slight, Emma is jubilant. "Never had she been more surprised, seldom more delighted, than at that instant. She was all pleasure and gratitude, ... and longed to be thanking him; and though too distant for speech, her countenance said much, as soon as she could catch his eye again" (328). Even here, where Emma is delighting in his attention to her own star pupil, we are reminded of her subconscious love by a hint of jealousy: "Harriet would have seemed almost too lucky, if it had not been for the cruel state of things before" (328).

The culmination of all these arguments, the pedagogic battles and the latent love, is of course the Miss Bates incident. It is the emotional climax of the novel. Mr. Knightly believes Emma will very soon marry his rival, but claims his privilege for the last time—"once more"—of remonstrating when he sees her acting wrongly. "Emma recollected, blushed, was sorry, but tried to laugh it off" (374)—the usual pattern. He persists in his reproach, however, and this time deeply disturbs her—"she felt it at her heart" (376). But there is no time for placation or reconciliation, and after the hurried parting, Emma is utterly desolate. All her confidence in her own judgement, her perseverance in her own courses, her determination not to give in, are done away with. She mends her ways and calls on Miss Bates, rather hoping Mr. Knightley will find her so creditably occupied: "She had no objection. She would not be ashamed of the appearance of the penitence, so justly and truly hers" (377-8). She is a new Emma. And when Mr. Knightley does understand she has learned her lesson and is not resentful, it is a moment of full and loving accord, and physically expressed:

> He looked at her with a glow of regard.... He took her hand;—whether she had not herself made the first motion, she could not say—she might, perhaps, have rather offered it—but he took her hand, pressed it, and certainly was on the point of carrying it to his lips. (385-6)

Emma and Mr. Knightley have both more to learn about each other's feelings before that kiss can happen; but the spontaneous and simultaneous clasp of the hands, in the moment of harmony between master and pupil, is a memorable image for the mutually passionate and joyful commitment implied in the pedagogic relationship in Jane Austen's novels.

Emma's and Mr. Knightley's love has grown and been manifested in their relations as master and pupil. When Emma discovers her love for him, it is in terms of his teaching role: "He had loved her, and watched over her from a girl, with an endeavour to improve her, and an anxiety for her doing right, which no other creature had at all shared" (415); and when he avows his love for her, it is in the same terms; "You hear nothing but truth from me.—I have blamed you, and lectured you, and you have borne it as no other woman in England would have borne it" (430). Mind and heart have been fully and simultaneously involved, so that the love has found its existence and expression through the teaching and the learning. In Mr. Knightley's case, by his own avowal, it is the love that has taken precedence of the education: "My interference was quite as likely to do harm as good.... The good was all to myself, by making you an object of the tenderest affection to me" (462).

In *Persuasion* it is the hero who must learn, while the heroine remains morally static. But we do not have a full reversal of the Emma-Mr. Knightley situation, in that Anne teaches Wentworth not by precept but by example, so that she doesn't really qualify for the pedagogue's role in that relation. As in *Pride and Prejudice*, the principals of this novel are in a sense antagonists—Wentworth is determined to stay angry with Anne as Elizabeth is determined to dislike Darcy—but here we have no merry war. The "perpetual estrangement" (64) is a cause not of merriment but of pain, and gives the novel its emotional poignancy. Anne is isolated from the man she loves, and can neither influence him nor be influenced by him for much of the novel. This estrangement is emphasized by the fact that hero and heroine—briefly and abortively—set up pedagogic relations elsewhere.

As we have seen, Wentworth takes on the role of pedagogue for his other woman: and being offended by Anne's persuasability, lectures Louisa on the virtues of firmness: "My first wish for all, whom I am interested in, is that they should be firm" (88). The misguided teacher finds an enthusiastic pupil, and Louisa, "being now armed with the idea of merit in maintaining her own way" (94), insists on going to Lyme, insists on being jumped from stiles, insists on leaping from the Cobb. "I am determined I will," she declares (109)—and so she comes a cropper.

In the interval Anne has become instructress for another man too, the bereaved Captain Benwick, who like her is grieving over a lost love. She gives him a bracing lecture on fortitude, and, "feeling in herself the right of seniority of mind," directs him to read "such works of our best moralists... as occurred to her at the moment as calculated to rouse and fortify the mind by the highest precepts" (101). She is not without a wry sense of the irony of her role as instructress:

> Anne could not but be amused at the idea of her coming to Lyme, to preach patience and resignation to a young man whom she had never seen before; nor could she help fearing, on more serious reflection, that, like many other great moralists and preachers, she had been eloquent on a point in which her own conduct would ill bear examination. (101)

For all this, Benwick responds as warmly to her instructions as Louisa does to Wentworth's, and seems so ready and eager to be consoled that he is in a fair way to forgetting his lost fiancée in falling in love with Anne.

However, by that symmetrical re-coupling caused by the accident on the

Cobb, the two facile pupils are thrown together and very plausibly united, so clearing away at least some of the obstacles between their instructors.

> [Anne] saw no reason against their being happy.... They would soon grow more alike. He would gain cheerfulness, and she would learn to be an enthusiast for Scott and Lord Byron; nay, that was probably learnt already; of course they had fallen in love over poetry. (167)

There is a little history in miniature of a pedagogic relationship, stripped of the perils and pitfalls encountered by more complex souls like Elizabeth, Darcy and Emma.

Anne has not been Wentworth's instructress, except indirectly in the scene where he overhears her fervent speech on constancy; but she has been the occasion of his learning. He tells her how at Lyme he had "received lessons of more than one sort.... There, he had learnt to distinguish between the steadiness of principle and the obstinacy of self-will" (242). Anne is more fortunate than many a teacher in being able to claim, "I must believe that I was right, much as I suffered from it" (246). But Wentworth, like Darcy who must learn to be laughed at, is to continue his education: "I must learn to brook being happier than I deserve" (247). It is a propitious ending.

Jane Austen has greater faith than most writers in the love fully combined with knowledge of self and esteem for the partner that is implied in her version of the pedagogic relationship. That mutual contribution to the formation of character, that mingling of minds as well as hearts and bodies, is joyful and totally fulfilling. But in Jane Austen there is always a qualification. I have been talking about the pedagogic relationship in its successful operation, as it occurs between hero and heroine, with its emotional and sexual implications. But it is not always successful. And Jane Austen examines with a critical eye both the right of one mind to influence another, and the complicity of the mind that allows itself to be influenced. She is fully aware of the possible arrogance of the pedagogic enterprise between fallible human beings: we need only remember Emma and Harriet. She occasionally endorses Elizabeth's touch of cynicism (it is before Elizabeth learns that she had indeed taught Darcy a lesson): "We all love to instruct, though we can teach only what is not worth knowing" (*PP*, 343). And she gives full attention to the mischief done by misguided mentors, however well-intentioned, like Sir Thomas Bertram and Mrs. Norris, and finally says of the original Persuader, "There was nothing less for Lady Russell to do, than to admit that she had been pretty completely wrong, and to take up a new set of opinions and hopes" (*P*, 249).

"Persuasion" is an issue not only in the last novel. Darcy's control of Bingley, Emma's of Harriet, Mary's of Edmund, are critically examined and the characters are judged—as arrogant, as pliable, as silly, in their different degrees. Ultimately Jane Austen insists that richly as a pupil may receive, or disastrously as he may be misled, he is responsible. He cannot be a mere passive receptacle of wisdom, or a mere victim of bad advice. The pupil makes his choices—he may choose or not choose to be instructed; he may elect his instructor; he may select which of the instructions to attend to. In all these choices he defines himself, and he has himself to accuse if they are wrong. There can be no shrugging off the blame. Emma is blameworthy in her influence on Harriet, and is certainly fortunate that Robert Martin is so manfully persistent as to get Harriet in the end anyway; but then Harriet had no business allowing Emma to run her life for her in the first place; and, had he lost her, Martin's loss would have been so much the less. This issue of responsibility is fully explored in *Mansfield Park*, where Edmund tries to excuse Mary's behaviour by putting the blame on her education, and at last extorts Fanny's impatient outburst, "Her friends leading her astray for years! She is quite as likely to have led *them* astray" (*MP*, 424). Jane Fairfax carefully avoids Edmund's kind of injustice in her apology to Mrs. Weston: "Do not imagine, madam,... that I was taught wrong. Do not let any reflection fall on the principles or the care of the friends who brought me up. The error has been all my own" (*E*, 419). It is a noble declaration: a brave and full acceptance of responsibility.

Embedded in all Jane Austen's novels is a pedagogic story, a story not just of learning—most novels are that—but of teaching too. We see courses of instruction proceeding through initiation, lectures, examination, graduation, qualification. We hear of pupils apt, and too eager, and recalcitrant; of teachers discerning, misguided, perverse. All of this bears much of the moral import of the novels, as the reader learns along with the lecturers and the students. But it also carries the emotional interest, as hero and heroine respond to each other, fully and consciously, come to share their experience, their feelings, and themselves, and are thus wholly united. T. S. Eliot[15] would perhaps disclaim the analogy, but it seems to me that the "felt thought" that he finds as the characteristic of metaphysical poetry has some kinship with the "intelligent love" that Lionel Trilling finds as Jane Austen's ideal. She too presents an intense and simultaneous commitment of feeling and intelligence, and her novels within their sphere dramatize the achievement of that commitment. She shows us what is for her the most passionate love, a love that is fully aware. Emma comes to realize that her first endeavour must be "to understand, thoroughly understand her own heart" (*E*, 412). There is no need to apologize for the spinster Jane, even though she may never show us her lovers in bed. In the fullest sense, she *understood* love, and made sure her best men and women come to do so too.

CHAPTER IV

Love and Marriage

Mr. Bennet, we hear late in *Pride and Prejudice*, "captivated by youth and beauty, and that appearance of good humour, which youth and beauty generally give, had married a woman whose weak understanding and illiberal mind, had very early in their marriage put an end to all real affection for her" (236). It takes an effort of mind to remember that the cerebral ironist we have come to know could originally have been "captivated by youth and beauty," betrayed into a disastrous marriage by his senses and the desire of the flesh. But it is an essential piece of information. The Bennet marriage must be accounted for, and Jane Austen lets us know the original motivation. The modern student may laugh at the quaintly formal usage of "Mr. Bennet" and "Mrs. Bennet" in the couple's conversation, and find it difficult to image such partners in bed. But the Bennets had five children, after all. And even at the novel's opening, it would seem, Mr. Bennet has a coltish tooth. He tells his wife that there is no need for him to visit Mr. Bingley:

> "You and the girls may go, or you may send them by themselves, which perhaps will be still better, for as you are as handsome as any of them, Mr. Bingley might like you the best of the party."
> "My dear, you flatter me. I certainly *have* had my share of beauty, but I do not pretend to be any thing extraordinary now. When a woman has five grown up daughters, she ought to give over thinking of her own beauty."
> "In such cases, a woman has not often much beauty to think of." (4)

That passage can be read as just one more of Mr. Bennet's cruel sallies against his wife—particularly cruel in that he pays her an apparent compliment and then ridicules her for being gratified at a mockery. But I prefer to read it straight, as a moment of rather touching self-awareness on Mr. Bennet's part, not a trap for his all too gullible wife. Perhaps she *is* still in his eyes as handsome as any of his daughters, and he recognizes his own susceptibility, like a kind of weary Samson contemplating his Delilah.

If he married her for her beauty, she married him for his estate. Her disillusion has been parallel with his—as he discovered her beauty insufficient compensation for her weak mind, she has found the entail on the estate likely to cancel out the estate itself. *Luxuria* for the man, *cupiditas* for the woman—it is a frequent though not invariable alignment. So with the Bertrams: "About thirty years ago, Miss Maria Ward of Huntingdon, with only seven thousand pounds, had the good luck to captivate Sir Thomas Bertram, of Mansfield Park,... and to be thereby raised to the rank of a baronet's lady, with all the comforts and consequences of an handsome house and large income" (*MP*, 3). So with Isabella Thorpe, Lucy Steele, Charlotte Lucas and Maria Bertram. The mercenary marriage motive, so evident in Jane Austen's novels, has been very sufficiently discussed.[1] But though she is less explicit about the sexual motive, she equally recognizes it as a major operating force. And it operates with the women as well as the men. Mark Schorer has characterized *Pride and Prejudice* as "a novel about marriage as a market, and about the female as marketable."[2] The poster for the Olivier/Garson screen adaptation of the novel, on the other hand, says it is about "how five love-hungry beauties find husbands!" While I would want to be more moderate than the poster (though husbands for Mary and Kitty would certainly gratify me) I too want to emphasize the erotic rather than the economic motive for marriage in Jane Austen's novels.

Mrs. Bennet's eldest daughter, Jane, has both the youth and beauty and the genuine good humour of which youth and beauty are only an appearance. Mr. Bingley, in being so early captivated by Jane, is another Mr. Bennet, but he will not be disillusioned like his father-in-law, because here the beauty and good humour unite—of Jane he may justifiably say, Behold the first in virtue as in face. Jane is no coquette, and she is quite incapable of practising the arts that Charlotte Lucas recomends: "In nine cases out of ten, a woman had better shew *more* affection than she feels" (22). But nevertheless Jane Austen can show how she makes her beauty effective. There is a pleasant mixture of consciousness and spontaneity in her by which we can see how Bingley is charmed: when he is uncertain whether he should sit by her at the dinner at Longbourn, "On entering the room, he seemed to hesitate; but Jane happened to look round, and happened to smile: it was decided. He placed himself by her" (340). Jane Austen can convey very well that physical magnetism that is so basic an element of courtship.

Though Jane's attraction is exerted effortlessly and almost unconsciously, other women use their sex more deliberately as a baited hook. How much Jane Austen knows about the flirt! Here is Isabella Thorpe, with her crudely mannered posturings, trying to snare a richer catch than her current fiancé. She fixes her eye on Captain Tilney until he notices her, and engages him in the language of flirtation.

"You men have none of you any hearts."

"If we have not hearts, we have eyes; and they give us torment enough."

"Do they? I am sorry for it; I am sorry they find any thing so disagreeable in me. I will look another way. I hope this pleases you, (turning her back on him), I hope your eyes are not tormented now."

"Never more so; for the edge of a blooming cheek is still in view—at once too much and too little."

Catherine heard all this, and quite out of countenance could listen no longer. (*NA*, 147)

One sympathizes with Catherine—it is hackneyed stuff. But that threadbare romantic jargon—hearts, eyes, torments—is captured perfectly, and we watch the seamy little game of sexual tantalizing ("at once too much and too little"), played by a man and woman both perfectly cynical about romance, but watching for their respective advantage: a better catch for the woman, another conquest for the man. Tilney wins. Isabella is not clever enough to make him marry her, and by his calculated flirtation—the whispered intimacies, the verbal sex play—he has at least made her enough his own that her legitimate fiancé relinquishes her.

In Lucy Steele's engagement to Edward Ferrars we see an instance of the woman's victory. By her youth and her wiles, she has him fairly caught, and she doesn't care how he writhes and thrashes on the hook. We don't see the process of her angling, nor the display of her bait and lures as we do with Isabella, but she speaks the same hackneyed romantic language to convince Elinor of his lasting love for her. In the present of the ring with her hair that Edward is obliged to wear, and in her display of trophies—his picture, his letter—we see something of her tactics. There is something particularly repellent about Lucy in her insistent confidences to Elinor on her love life. She is not simply protecting her own, she is deliberately wounding her rival in the gratuitous revelation of her engagement: "She looked down as she said this, amiably bashful, with only one side glance at her companion to observe its effect on her" (*SS*, 129). One is momentarily reminded of Coleridge's Geraldine, the serpent woman, first "in maiden wise / Casting down her large bright eyes," and then glancing sideways at Christabel:

> A snake's small eye blinks dull and shy;
> And the lady's eyes they shrunk in her head,
> Each shrunk up to a serpent's eye,
> And with somewhat of malice, and more of dread,
> At Christabel she looked askance! (*Christabel*, 573-587)

Jane Austen doesn't create lamias, and she never shows us Lucy's wrinkled bosom and scaly sides as Coleridge does Geraldine's. But she can on occasion create a quite sufficiently nasty antagonist for her women, and generate the kind of repugnance we usually expect as a reaction to villains of romance. Edward, like Christabel's suitor on whom Geraldine has designs, is bewitched by Lucy, who is his Geraldine, his Duessa. He is another of the men who has been "captivated" by the outward and physical attractions of youth and beauty.

In Caroline Bingley we see another unsuccessful attempt at captivation. She is not so prominent in *Pride and Prejudice* as Lucy Steele is in the previous novel, but in the constant failures of her schemes to catch Darcy she gives the reader much of the rather primitive pleasure of rejoicing in the fall of an enemy—the more so because Elizabeth herself cares so little for her success or failure. When Darcy admits to finding pleasure in a pair of fine eyes in the face of a pretty woman, "Miss Bingley immediately fixed her eyes on his face, and desired he would tell her what lady had the credit of inspiring such reflections." At Darcy's answer, "Miss Elizabeth Bennet," the reader must rejoice at Miss Bingley's discomfiture (27). But her campaign proceeds, and in echoing all his statements, choosing the second volume of his book for her own reading, and abusing Elizabeth, she offers a fine range of tactics. Darcy's definitive speech on them is another of those gratifying moments that the reader savours, if not Elizabeth:

> "Eliza Bennet," said Miss Bingley, when the door was closed on her, "is one of those young ladies who seek to recommend themselves to the other sex, by undervaluing their own; and with many men, I dare say, it succeeds. But, in my opinion, it is a paltry device, a very mean art."
> "Undoubtedly," replied Darcy, to whom this remark was chiefly addressed, "there is meanness in *all* the arts which ladies sometimes condescend to employ for captivation. Whatver bears affinity to cunning is despicable."
> Miss Bingley was not so entirely satisfied with this reply as to continue the subject. (*PP*, 40)

There is no comparably satisfying put-down of the Blanche Ingrams of Charlotte Brontë's novels.

Emma's flirting with Frank Churchill on Box Hill is virtually devoid of sexual content, at least for the principals. Their language of flirtation is a kind of intellectual exercise, and their display is entirely for the benefit of other people rather than for each other. Emma self-consciously reflects that her behaviour "in the judgment of most people looking on ... must have had such an appearance as no English word but flirtation could very well describe" (*E*, 368). But Frank's flirting, at least, is a deliberate ploy to wound Jane Fairfax, in which he fully succeeds. Mr. Knightley likewise looks on in pain, and concludes that Emma is finally lost to him. So the publicity of this flirtation is of its essence.

Jane Austen's strong sense of the community's concern in a courtship makes her good at depicting the phase of love in which an audience is required. Louisa Musgrove's harmless flirting with Wentworth—harmless compared with Isabella's or Lucy's flirting, which is a deliberate strategy—can be done best in the midst of people. It even helps her that at the outset her sister is joined in the flirtation—her innocence in the eyes of the world is thus assured, and she can thereby let her "little fever of admiration" develop into love. She could not have physical contact with Wentworth in private—their relationship has not reached that stage. But in the family party she can insist that he jump her down from stiles, for "the sensation was delightful to her" (*P*, 109). As usual, Jane Austen is acutely aware of the physical constituent in the relations between her men and women. Here, although Wentworth has said nothing of love or marriage to Louisa, he finds that their harmless dalliance before spectators, his "excessive intimacy," has in effect committed him to marrying her if she wants him. The sexual lures have been placed, though in this case unconsciously, and the man has been caught. "I was hers in honour if she wished it," he reflects afterwards (*P*, 242).

Though much of the sexual aspect of courtship is suggested rather than described, the novels are quite sufficiently stored with evidence of the physical attraction between the major characters. The men, as one would expect, are more ready to expatiate on the beauties of their women than vice versa. Those who find Jane Austen spinsterish and niggardly of lovers' raptures may need reminding of Frank Churchill's running commentary to Emma on his fiancée's beauty: "Look at her.... Observe the turn of the throat. Observe her eyes, as she is looking up at my father.—You will be glad to hear (inclining his head, and whispering seriously) that my uncle means to give her all my aunt's jewels. They are to be new set. I am resolved to have some in an ornament for the head. Will not it be beautiful in her dark hair?" (*E*, 479). The parenthesis about Frank's seriousness is no doubt a reminder of the slightly amused perspective we are to maintain on this outpouring. But the outpouring in itself is sympathetically done, and is evidence quite sufficient of Frank's passionate appreciation of Jane's beauty.

We hear enough, too, to be satisfied of Darcy's response to Elizabeth's magnetism, which is physical as well as temperamental. Against all his resolutions, he finds his eyes drawn to her—as in the scene when Miss Bingley, who has not been able to draw his attention from his book by her own pacing up and down the room, invites Elizabeth to join her: "Mr.

Darcy looked up ... and unconsciously closed his book" (56). The unwillingness of his attentions of course for the reader adds immeasurably to their interest. His "In vain have I struggled" speech (189) is as well calculated to stir romantic feeling as Mr. Rochester's "God pardon me! ... and man meddle not with me: I have her, and will hold her" (*Jane Eyre*, Ch. 23). I find it interesting, and no slur on either novel, that schoolgirls tend to fall in love with Darcy as readily as with Rochester.[3]

Wentworth's susceptibility to Anne is manifested chiefly in his jealousy of Mr. Elliot at Bath. Although more than one of Jane Austen's lovers are put to the pain of seeing the women they love courted by other men—Brandon, and more notably Knightley—it is in Wentworth that we most clearly see the pangs of jealousy. As usual the point of view is centred in the woman, but we can deduce Wentworth's feelings from his motions during the concert —diverging from his straight course through the room to speak to her; withdrawing as she is drawn into the circle of her family and Mr. Elliot; watching as her attention is claimed by Elliot, and her curiosity roused by his tantalizing reference to his early knowledge of her character; drawn back by her manoeuvring to contemplate sitting next to her; and withdrawing again in haste when Elliot again solicits her attention. His irritable opinion that the music is bad and the gathering tedious is all due to the state of his emotions, his conviction that Elliot's chances with Anne are better than his. "To see your cousin close by you, conversing and smiling, and feel all the horrible eligibilities and properties of the match! ... How could I look on without agony?" he exclaims to Anne afterwards (*P*, 244). And it is a satisfaction here to find Anne, even the strongly principled Anne, briefly enjoying the pleasure of prompting his jealousy: "For a moment the gratification was exquisite" (191). She has endured so much herself.

When we turn to the woman's susceptibility to the man's attractions, it is obviously useful to consider the tactics of the seducer, since his success must be in the teeth of all social restrictions.

Willoughby is the actual seducer of Miss Williams, and the potential seducer of Marianne. In his energetic pursuit of Marianne he cooly waits to see how far he can go in engaging her love, without getting himself entangled. "I endeavoured," he admits to Elinor, "by every means in my power, to make myself pleasing to her, without any design of returning her affection" (*SS*, 320). The means in his power are considerable. He has the initial advantage of their close physical contact at the outset: "Marianne herself had seen less of his person that the rest, for the confusion which crimsoned over her face, on his lifting her up, had robbed her of the power of regarding him after their entering the house. But she had seen enough of him to join in all the admiration of the others, and with an energy which always adorned her praise" (43). Marianne is as little impervious to being carried in a handsome man's arms as Hardy's farm girls, Retty, Izz, and another Marian, in that similarly titillating incident in *Tess of the D'Ubervilles* (Ch. 23). And Marianne is closer to being the victim of a seducer than any other heroine, for we learn enough of her readiness for illicit encounters and clandestine journeys, like the trip to Allenham, to suppose that she is in real danger. I take the scene of the rape of the lock, as described to Elinor by Margaret, to be an emblem of things possibly to come:

> "Last night after tea, when you and mama went out of the room, they were whispering and talking together as fast as could be, and he seemed to be begging something of her, and presently he took up her scissars and cut off a long lock of her hair, for it was all tumbled down her back; and he kissed it, and folded it up in a piece of white paper, and put it into his pocket-book." (60)

The tumbled hair, the reluctantly granted boon, the kissing and triumphant appropriation of the lock, all suggest that Marianne might yield to seduction: her principle, since she asserts that the pleasantness of an occupation is evidence of its propriety (68), would hardly save her from Miss Williams' fate. Willoughby claims that for a while he did intend to ask her to marry him. But essentially it is the discovery of the last seduction that terminates his next attempt.

Wickham is more facile and less dangerous. His attempt at seducing Georgiana Darcy is abortive, and his actual seduction of Lydia is as much a triumph for her as for him. Elizabeth at the first encounter is ready to be charmed by him, for "his appearance was greatly in his favour; he had all the best part of beauty, a fine countenance, a good figure, and very pleasing address" (*PP*, 72). But her favourable first impression, prompted by his unsolicited confidences, is warm enough only to make her unguardedly partisan in taking up his cause; she is never in danger of being fully captivated, as she shows by her good-humoured acceptance of Mrs. Gardiner's cautions, and her calm tolerance of Wickham's attentions to Miss King. Her interest in him is really subordinate to her interest in Darcy, and she cultivates him and his spurious revelations because Darcy has already engaged her attention. The most intimate physical contact between them is after she knows all about his deceptions, and has shown she knows. "She held out her hand; he kissed it with affectionate gallantry, though he hardly knew how to look" (329). And his constant exertions to please, and to get something by pleasing, are finally comic, as they become mere grist to the mill of Mr. Bennet's appetite for the ridiculous: "He is as fine a fellow . . . as ever I saw.

He simpers, and smirks, and makes love to us all. I am prodigiously proud of him" (330).

Henry Crawford is much more dangerous. His motivation is more complex than Wickham's: he is not simply seeking to advance himself in the world, for his dangerous liaisons are usually against his own best interests. Given a choice between two sisters, one free and one engaged, he perversely picks the engaged one; and as soon as he has a real prospect of winning the woman he loves, he turns away to pursue a married woman whom he has already dropped once.[4] It is presumably an enormous vanity that creates his need to make a hole in every woman's heart, particularly if the woman appears difficult of conquest. But his talents in love-making are much greater than Wickham's though not so indiscriminately applied. He is persistently intimate, determinedly confidential. He finds pretexts for holding hands, for innuendoes, for whispered conversations, for looks of meaning. He is in his proper element during the theatricals at Mansfield Park, because there he can do his love-making and rehearse his passionate scenes without any commitment. He and Maria are "indefatigable rehearsers" (*MP*, 169) of their roles as Frederick and Agatha. And when the rehearsing is so dramatically interrupted by the arrival of Sir Thomas, Maria understandably sets much store by the fact that Henry, in the midst of the general consternation, keeps her hand pressed to his heart, even though the rehearsal is over and real life is again in progress. The circumstance "was to her the sweetest support. Henry Crawford's retaining her hand at such a moment, a moment of such peculiar proof and importance, was worth ages of doubt and anxiety" (176). Jane Austen may not go far in the depiction of physical love, but the hand-clasps and interrupted kisses are certainly made to carry a full load of significance. In this case, Henry Crawford accomplishes the seduction of Maria's feelings, if not her body. It is such a triumph as he delights in. Maria is wrenched from her mercenary motive by her passion, from her "Rushworth-feelings" by her "Crawford-feelings" (81); and he himself is heartwhole and unentangled. He has no such feelings as Wentworth about being "hers in honour if she wished it." His innuendoes and play-acted lovemaking serve their purpose of ensnaring others without committing him.

Crawford we know has "moral taste" (235)—not a sufficient substitute for principle, but still a quality important in him, both in that it makes him able to appreciate Fanny, and in that it enables him to recommend himself to her. He employs his old tactics without effect—she is embarrassed by his softened voice and his covert gift of the necklace, and disappointed that his nimble attentiveness should prevent Edmund's putting her shawl round her shoulders (251). But his practice in such affairs is considerable, and his persistence along with his readiness to learn new tactics all have their effect. We get all the detail of his courtship, of which she is so involuntarily the object. When, determined not to enter conversation with him, she silently shakes her head at one of his comments, he is ready to overwhelm her with solicitous attentions:

> Crawford was instantly by her side again, intreating to know her meaning; and as Edmund perceived, by his drawing in a chair, and sitting down close by her, that it was to be a very thorough attack, that looks and undertones were to be well tried, he sank as quietly as possible into a corner, turned his back, and took up a newspaper, very sincerely wishing that dear little Fanny might be persuaded into explaining away that shake of the head to the satisfaction of her ardent lover. (341-2)

Crawford's adaptation of his usual tactics is to profess to be influenced for good by Fanny, to see himself as she sees him, to understand his faults and reform them. "You think me unsteady—easily swayed by the whim of the moment—easily tempted—easily put aside. With such an opinion, no wonder that—but we shall see.... My conduct shall speak for me" (343). He throws himself into this part as enthusiastically as into all his others, and he has shrewdly hit on just the right method of flattering Fanny—which is not easily done. To show himself merely as her ardent admirer, as he did to Maria, avails nothing. But to show himself as influenced to good by her, as ready to go back to his estate and look after his poor but honest tenants,— that comes near to touching her heart. He might well have made that hole in it, but for Edmund.

Of course it is not only to the masculine charms of the practised and deliberate seducers that Jane Austen's heroines are susceptible. We learn quite enough about their pleasure in proximity and contact with the men they love to know they are warm and responsive, and would by no means be the sort of brides who "closed their eyes and thought of England" in the marriage bed.[5] From the time Edmund gave her brotherly assistance in her childhood, Fanny is sensitive to his presence, appreciative of his proximity. Then he ruled her lines for her, and "continued with her the whole time of her writing, to assist her with his penknife or his orthography." These attentions, we know, "she felt very much" (16)—just as later she is to take particular pleasure in his placing her shawl round her shoulders. So it is when he stargazes with her: "Fanny... had the pleasure of seeing him continue at the window with her, in spite of the expected glee; and of having his eyes soon turned like her's towards the scene without, where all that was solemn and soothing, and lovely, appeared in the brilliancy of an unclouded night" (112-3). Edmund's proximity no doubt has some part in her rapture as she gazes at the starlit heavens.

Emma is acutely responsive to the sight of Knightley. Early in the novel, "as he stood up, in tall indignation," it is as though he momentarily fills her whole vision (60). And at the ball at the Crown she can hardly keep her eyes off him: "He could not have appeared to greater advantage perhaps any where, than where he had placed himself. His tall, firm, upright figure, among the bulky forms and stooping shoulders of the elderly men, was such as Emma felt must draw every body's eyes" (326). And then there is that beautifully planted clue about her feeling for him in the scene where Harriet is reminding her of the night Mr. Elton left his pencil stub:

> "I do remember it," cried Emma; "I perfectly remember it.—Talking about spruce beer....—Stop; Mr. Knightley was standing just here, was not he?—I have an idea he was standing just here."
> "Ah, I do not know. I cannot recollect....—Mr. Elton was sitting here, I remember, much about where I am now." (339-40)

It is a fine indication of the working of Emma's mind. She is evidently at all times subliminally conscious of Knightley's whereabouts and movements, to the extent that her memory retains the impression of his figure when most of the rest of the scene is forgotten.

Anne Elliot is similarly intent on Wentworth, though necessarily from a distance. She early discovers that he is as handsome as ever—"the years which had destroyed her youth and bloom had only given him a more glowing, manly, open look, in no respect lessening his personal advantages" (*P*, 61). Wentworth, with his glowing looks and glances of brightness, is associated with light and the sun, and is the cynosure of Anne's eyes. In this he is like Will Ladislaw, another romantic figure, who shakes sunlight from his curls. George Eliot's imagery is more insistent, but no more effective.

Anne has the particular pain of a special kind of intimacy: although they are, as she believes, perpetually estranged, she still knows the workings of his features well enough to be able to interpret his feelings better than anyone else. "There was a momentary expression in Captain Wentworth's face at this speech, a certain glance of his bright eye, and curl of his handsome mouth, which convinced Anne, that instead of sharing in Mrs. Musgrove's kind wishes, as to her son, he had probably been at some pains to get rid of him; but it was too transient an indulgence of self-amusement to be detected by any who understood him less than herself" (67). This intentness of scrutiny and minuteness of observation are frequently noticeable in the novel, for in the intervals of Anne's watchfulness of Wentworth, Wentworth is often watching her—he is the only one to perceive, for instance, her fatigue after the walk to Winthrop, and so he can take action for her relief.

In a discussion of the erotic response of Jane Austen's women to their men, it is worth considering her use of the rescue, which is often a stimulus to love. The hero's rescue of the heroine has been a standard ingredient of romance no doubt since well before Lancelot snatched Guinevere from the stake, and it has become a staple of melodrama and movie romances. Charlotte Brontë, a stouter feminist than Jane Austen, bravely reversed the stereotype, and has Jane Eyre rescue Rochester—she helps him when he has sprained his ankle (*pace* Willoughby!), and douses the fire in his bed. Jane Austen's rescues, as might be expected, are less spectacular; but they are there nonetheless, and they often have a profound effect on the heroine's feelings. The instance of Wentworth's consideration for Anne on the Winthrop walk is a case in point. He leaps over a hedge to let the Crofts know that Anne needs a ride home, whereupon the Crofts very kindly urge her to get into their carriage. Anne is deeply moved.

> Yes,—he had done it. She was in the carriage, and felt that he had placed her there, that his will and his hands had done it, that she owed it to his perception of her fatigue, and his resolution to give her rest. She was very much affected by the view of his disposition towards her which all these things made apparent. (91)

This is hardly a rescue by a knight on a dashing white charger; but the moment is fraught with emotion. Wordsworth's "little, nameless, unremembered, acts / Of kindness and of love" are here fleshed out, and become memorable and momentous.

Perhaps the most powerful rescue scene in the novels (and there are many, though of varying intensity) is also in *Persuasion*: Anne's deliverance by Wentworth from the tiresome little Walter Musgrove. I think most people respond keenly to this scene, though without recognizing its standard romance component of the rescue. But here, because it is too good to miss, I quote Maurice Zapp, the genial English professor in David Lodge's novel, who thus enlightens his students:

> Readers of Jane Austen, he emphasized, gesturing freely with his cigar, should not be misled by the absence of overt reference to physical sexuality in her fiction into supposing that she was indifferent or hostile to it. On the contrary, she invariably came down on the side of Eros against Agape. ... Getting into his stride, Morris demonstrated that Mr Elton was obviously implied to be impotent because there was no lead in the pencil that Harriet Smith took from him; and the moment in *Persuasion* when Captain Wentworth lifted the little brat Walter off Anne Elliot's shoulders. ... He snatched up the text and read with feeling:

> "... she found herself in the state of being released from him ... Before she realized that Captain Wentworth had done it ... he was resolutely borne away ... Her sensations on the discovery made her perfectly speechless. She could not even thank him. She could only hang over little Charles with the most disordered feelings. How about that?" he concluded reverently. "If that isn't an *orgasm*, what is it?" He looked up into three flabbergasted faces.[6]

It is mortifying to be so anticipated, not to say parodied in advance. But I must contend all the same that Professor Zapp is on to something. Jane Austen's women respond with deeply-felt excitement at such moments. They are moments that create or confirm love. As Emma knowingly tells Harriet, "The service he rendered you was enough to warm your heart."

> "Service! [replies Harriet] oh! it was such in inexpressible obligation! —The very recollection of it, and all that I felt at the time—when I saw him coming—his noble look—and my wretchedness before. Such a change! In one moment such a change! From perfect misery to perfect happiness."
> (*E*, 342)

It might be Rebecca responding when Sir Wilfred of Ivanhoe gallops into the lists to be her champion. However, as readers will remember, there is a serious muddle here between Emma and Harriet: the "service" Emma has in mind is Frank's, in rescuing Harriet from the gipsies, but Harriet is thinking of Mr. Knightley's timely invitation to dance when Elton has slighted her at the Crown ball. The muddle suggests that there are two kinds of rescue, the genuine and the spurious, and only one is the kind that arouses and deserves love. The spurious ones are such as are the staple of the usual romance, and are matters merely of chance: Frank in the incident with the gipsies, Willoughby at the scene of the sprained ankle, and Mr. Dixon in the boat at Weymouth, merely happen to be there, and, being there, do the obvious thing. Not on such fortuitous occurrences should a genuine love be based. The *real* rescue, the one that deserves the return of love, is a moral act, a matter of choice, like Wentworth's with Anne and little Walter, or Knightley's with Harriet on the dance floor. In both cases there are other people present who could have helped but didn't; it is the hero's heroism that moves him. On this point, Harriet's response is truer than Emma's on her behalf. *Harriet* knows the difference, and is quite unmoved by Frank's chasing off the gipsies.

Just as Harriet is one of the girls who, once she has begun, must always be in love, so she is one who is frequently being rescued. Mr. Knightley's and Frank's rescues are both anticipated by that of Robert Martin, who, notwithstanding her refusal of his proposal, kindly urges his sister to talk to her when she is stranded in Ford's by the rain, and bears her comfort in mind in advising her of the best route to Hartfield through the puddles.

"I had not got three yards from the door, when he came after me, only to say, if I was going to Hartfield, he thought I had much better go round by Mr. Cole's stables, for I should find the near way quite floated by this rain. Oh! dear, I thought it would be the death of me!... Oh, Miss Woodhouse, I would rather done any thing than have had it happen: and yet, you know, there was a sort of satisfaction in seeing him behave so pleasantly and so kindly." (179)

Harriet in this matter is as accessible to feeling as Anne, who feels a similar combination of pleasure and pain at Wentworth's acts of consideration. And Harriet's heart, like Anne's, is essentially pre-empted (for all her wavering) by this first rescue. This offended lover also loves her enough to ask her again.

Her handling of the rescue scene is one more example of Jane Austen's marvellous ability to domesticate romance, to bring it home, within the range of ordinary people living everyday lives. You don't have to be a Guinevere or a Rebecca to experience the intensity of that relief and exaltation in deliverance from pain by another's act of courage. The mind is its own place, and if you possess the capacity to feel intensely, the stimulus will not be wanting. Romance—the genuine kind, that depends on character rather than circumstance—is within reach.

"My child," pleads Mr. Bennet in one of the most moving moments of *Pride and Prejudice*, when he thinks Elizabeth intends to marry Darcy only for the prestige of his position, "let me not have the grief of seeing *you* unable to respect your partner in life" (376). It is the italic *"you"* that gives the advice its poignancy. This is a (for once) gently oblique reference to his own unhappy marriage. His own painfully achieved experience prompts his special concern for the marital fate of his favourite daughter when he sees her, as he thinks, following in his own footsteps.

Elizabeth and the reader know that the Darcy marriage will be far from a repetition of the Bennet one. But the Bennet marriage, and the other marriages in the novels, serve as present reminders of what marriage can be, as images of the ways in which that final happy consummation that the hero and heroine achieve can be for others, and potentially for them, a joyful partnership, or a prolonged humiliation, or a blind alley. The young heroine who makes her progress towards union with the hero is confronted with many previews of her own potential fate in the marriages of the older characters who surround her; and in this way we are given some inklings of the possibilities beyond the limits of the last page. We know that Jane Austen doesn't follow her girls beyond the altar; but we have enough present evidence to know that she could have if she had wanted to.

Other marriages that are explicitly marked out as possibilities for the heroine are those of the suitors she herself has rejected. Elizabeth, when she visits the Collinses at Hunsford, "could not help fancying that in displaying the good proportion of the room, its aspect and its furniture, [Mr. Collins] addressed himself particularly to her, as if wishing to make her feel what she had lost in refusing him" (*PP*, 156). Emma, as she watches the Eltons, can congratulate herself that she never had any intention of becoming Mrs. Elton. And Anne, when she enters the Musgrove house as Charles's sister-in-law, cannot but recollect she might have been there as his wife; though his talents are not such as "to make the past, as they were connected together, at all a dangerous contemplation" (*P*, 43). But by extension all the marriages become commentaries on the heroine's, and on each other. It is part of the marvellous interconnectedness within each novel that so little is irrelevant, so much invites significant comparison and contrast.

The range of existing marriages in the novels is considerable. Some are disasters: the Willoughbys and the Wickhams are apt to proceed to separation or divorce, like the Rushworths. The Palmers, who cause Elinor to muse over "the strange unsuitableness which often existed between husband and wife" (*SS*, 118), will perhaps settle into some such distant relationship as the Bennets. The Middletons seem to suit each other in their very distance, as his incorrigible sociability and her invariable insipidity drive them both to seek any company but each other's. Of Mrs. Allen in *Northanger Abbey* we hear that she "was one of that numerous class of females, whose society can raise no other emotion than of surprise at there being any men in the world who could like them well enough to marry them" (20). Such females are indeed numerous in the novels—Mrs. Allen is followed by Charlotte Palmer, Mrs. Bennet (though her stupidity is of a different order, and not manifested in placidity), and Lady Bertram. Anne de Bourgh is an as yet unmarried example of the same class.

Such a set of examples might well lead one to conclude with Mary Crawford that "there is not one in a hundred of either sex, who is not taken in when they marry.... It is, of all transactions, the one in which people expect most from others, and are least honest themselves.... It is a manoeuvring business" (*MP*, 46). There are passages in the letters that sound as though Jane Austen was close to sharing Mary's views. But in context Mary is told firmly, "Ah! You have been in a bad school for matrimony, in Hill Street." Her experience has shown her too exclusively the behaviour of her uncle and his circle. In fact the novels produce several examples of good and happy marriages: there is the comfortable compatibility of the Morlands and the Westons, the devotion of the Harvilles, and the cheerful partnership of the Crofts. Anne, in watching Mrs. Croft's judicious participation in her husband's driving, recognizes an emblem of their married life.

> By coolly giving the reins a better direction herself, they happily passed the danger; and by once afterwards judiciously putting out her hand, they neither fell into a rut, nor ran foul of a dung-cart; and Anne, with some amusement at their style of driving, which she imagined no bad representation of the general guidance of their affairs, found herself safely deposited by them at the cottage. (P, 92)

The two happiest of the marriages, of Harvilles and Crofts, are both in the last novel. There is some progression towards a mellower view of marriage and domesticity through the novels. In *Sense and Sensibility* one can discern a waspish tone, even a rather spinsterish intolerance of marriage and children. Lady Middleton's partiality for her horrid little brats is very severely handled, and the apparent fondness of the Misses Steele for the children has to be disgusting hypocrisy. But the view of marriage as exclusively a manoeuvring business is being discarded by the time it is put into Mary Crawford's mouth; and in *Persuasion*, where we hear in detail of the Harvilles' loving domestic arrangements, of the husband's and father's joy in being reunited with his loved ones, and of the pleasures of Christmas with the children at Uppercross, the scenes of love and marriage, home and children, are presented with deep sympathy. "Domestic virtues" are extolled in the final sentence of the novel.

The common factor among all these varying marriages is the view of marriage as a dynamic process, by which character continues to be moulded as the partners, for better or worse, accommodate and adapt to each other. When Anne contemplates Charles Musgrove, she reflects "that a more equal match might have greatly improved him; and that a woman of real understanding might have given more consequence to his character, and more usefulness, rationality, and elegance to his habits and pursuits" (43). To do him justice, Charles had tried to marry the right woman, Anne, but failing her, he settles for Mary, and as a result becomes merely a good-humoured trifler, who does nothing with much zeal but hunting, shooting and fishing.

John Dashwood similarly confirms his own worst tendencies by his marriage:

> He was not an ill-disposed man, unless to be rather cold hearted, and rather selfish, is to be ill-disposed.... Had he married a more amiable woman, he might have been made still more respectable than he was:—

he might even have been made more amiable himself; for he was very young when he married, and very fond of his wife. But Mrs. John Dashwood was a strong caricature of himself;—more narrow-minded and selfish. (*SS*, 5)

The process by which his wife, as the embodiment of his worser half, acts on him is memorably dramatized in the following chapter, in which he starts out by being reluctantly ready to bequeath his half-sisters a thousand pounds apiece, and under her prompting ends up by giving them nothing at all. It is a comic, but still sufficiently grim, version of the discussion between Goneril and Regan on Lear's hundred knights, which proceeds inexorably to the question, "What need one?" Husband and wife seek out their common ground, and confirm and reinforce one another, systematically renouncing all their duties to others, and reducing their sphere of responsibility to the tiny circle of themselves and little Harry.

Mr. Elton, like John Dashwood, is before marriage one of those blank quantities that have yet to be filled in according to the woman he marries. As Emma perceives, his will be an "Exactly so" marriage (*E*, 49), for his readiness in accommodation is considerable. If he had been able to marry Emma, as he intended, she would have been the dominant partner; if he had married Harriet, as Emma intended, the two malleable partners might have brought out each other's best qualities—Mr. Knightley acknowledges to Emma, "you would have chosen for him better than he has chosen for himself" (331); but in marrying Augusta Hawkins he too marries a strong caricature of his worst qualities. Presently we see them hunting in pairs, like the Dashwoods: when he insults Harriet, Emma "perceived that his wife ... was not only listening also, but even encouraging him by significant glances" (327). Elton is completed, almost created, by his marriage. Before it he was relatively an unknown quantity, a cipher awaiting the definitive addition of the significant numeral.

Jane Austen's married couples form a new amalgam, something that is more than the sum of its parts. To paraphrase Donne, marriage "interinanimates" two souls; and though the soul which thence doth flow is not necessarily "abler," it is at any rate a new entity, a third soul, product of a unique intimacy. Although she never gives us as detailed a scrutiny of a single marriage as we get, say, in *Vanity Fair* or *Middlemarch*, the many brief pictures of marriage nearly always give some indication of the working of this intimacy. Husband and wife are like Siamese twins, with a flow of blood between one another. James's conception of the Sacred Fount, by which one partner feeds off the other, is not more suggestive. In Jane Austen's novels the flow is not in one direction only, but the relation becomes as intimate and as definitive. And in the case of ill-matched couples, the lack of the exchange is as significant, for it is felt as a severing or a deprivation. Mr. and Mrs. Bennet may be poles apart, but they have become what they are largely because of each other.

The accommodation between husband and wife is not always for the worse. In the Collins marriage—another of the potential matches for the main character—the husband is lucky enough to have "met with one of the very few sensible women who would have accepted him, or have made him happy if they had" (*PP*, 178). Mr. Collins is too set in his ways—perhaps because his loyalties are already so engaged with Lady Catherine—to be much altered in himself, but Charlotte's constant alertness to cover up his worst excesses makes them as a couple almost tolerably sensible. Charlotte must do most of the accommodating. She cannot avoid wincing at some of his most embarrassing comments, "but in general Charlotte wisely did not hear" (156). Her marriage has involved the deliberate stifling of her perceptions; and her own household, which she has purchased at the price of such company, can be pleasant only on certain conditions: "When Mr. Collins could be forgotten, there was really a great air of comfort throughout, and by Charlotte's evident enjoyment of it, Elizabeth supposed he must be often forgotten" (157). It is not difficult to deduce that this state of deliberate insensibility extends to the marriage bed. Charlotte's is the most exclusively "prudential" marriage in the novels—there is no case of captivation on either side. She would be one of the few of Jane Austen's brides who would actually have needed to close their eyes and think of England on the marriage night.

The moral mingling that goes on in the Austen marriages is a correlative of physical union. Husband and wife are clearly one flesh. Jane Austen's fine sense of the rub of intimacy, of the way the constant contact in a close union produces sparks or smoothness, soreness or consonant grooves, is spelled out morally, but is also physically suggestive. We don't see Mr. and Mrs. Elton in bed, nor the Collinses, nor, fortunately, Sir Thomas and Lady Bertram. But we see the products of their intimacy, and, if our taste lies that way, it would not be difficult to construct plausible versions of their sex life. There is no doubt that it is there.

As I have shown in the last chapter, the heroine and hero have usually begun the process of adaptation and accommodation before marriage, and the giving and taking of moral knowledge has often created their love. But their happiness in marriage is recurrently seen as a continuation of this process; though the marriages of the principals usually differ from the marriages of minor characters in that there the change is to be joyfully mutual, and all for the better. Mr. Knightley finds in Emma "the open temper which a man would wish for in a wife" (288), and he has the moral judgement that she has had painfully to acquire. Her brother-in-law, she notes to Knightley, "is not without hope of my growing, in time, as worthy of your affection, as you think me already" (464)—to which Mr. Knightley loyally responds that he will soon convince his brother "of our having every right that equal worth can give, to be happy together" (465). Anne and Wentworth, through the course of *Persuasion*, similarly come to stand out as a kind of moral aristocracy of sense and sensibility, among the well-meaning but obtuse Musgroves or the unfeelingly snobbish Elliots: through a painful process they become fit for one another—though in this case Wentworth has had more to learn than Anne. At Lyme, he recalls, "he had learnt to distinguish between the steadiness of principle and the obstinacy of self-will, between the darings of heedlessness and the resolution of a collected mind" (*P*, 242): the faults he recognizes are not only Louisa's, but his own. Anne's virtues are to be the correction of his resentment, and the complement of his recklessness.

When Elizabeth is regretting her lost chance of marrying Darcy, she wryly reflects that "No such happy marriage could now teach the admiring multitude what connubial felicity really was." The marriage as she has just envisioned it is the clearest delineation of mutual enhancement in the novels. It is worth quoting again.

> She began now to comprehend that he was exactly the man, who, in disposition and talents, would most suit her. His understanding and temper, though unlike her own, would have answered all her wishes. It was an union that must have been to the advantage of both; by her ease and liveliness, his mind might have been softened, his manners improved, and from his judgment, information, and knowledge of the world, she must have received benefit of greater importance. (312)

This is the marriage that Elizabeth does achieve after all, and it is indeed one that can teach the admiring multitude what connubial felicity really is. This is not mere compatibility, but a full and mutual engagement and deployment of minds and hearts. Such too is to be the consummation achieved by Jane Eyre, as we are to understand from Rochester's final proposal:

"Jane suits me: do I suit her?"
"To the finest fibre of my nature, sir." (Ch. 37)

Jane Austen and Charlotte Brontë are not so different after all.

NOTES

FOREWORD

1. Contrast Annabella Milbanke on another novel: she wrote on reading *Pride and Prejudice* on its first emergence. "It is not a crying book, but the interest is very strong, especially for Mr. Darcy." The woman who was susceptible to Mr. Darcy two years later married Lord Byron. See Marghanita Laski, *Jane Austen and her World* (London, 1969), p. 86.
2. See *Jane Austen: The Critical Heritage*, ed. B.C. Southam (London, 1968), p. 128. I shall be returning to Charlotte Brontë's charges below, in Chapter II.
3. See "Apropos of *Lady Chatterley's Lover*" (1930).
4. See, for instance, Marjorie Proops: "Jane, the spinster daughter of a country Tory parson, ... ignored sex. At any rate, she threw a discreet veil over it.... She was a deeply religious woman and the physical consummation of love appeared to be outside her comprehension." *Pride, Prejudice and Proops* (London, 1975), pp. 11-12. Marjorie Proops can hardly be considered an expert on Jane Austen (she calls Darcy D'arcy, and thinks Jane Fairfax married Willoughby); but her silly little book is an interesting compendium of the popular modern clichés about Jane Austen.

CHAPTER I: THE SYMPTOMS OF LOVE

1. This was originally delivered as the address at the annual meeting of the Jane Austen Society in Chawton, Hampshire, on July 16, 1977. A version of the paper is published in the society's annual Report.
2. James Boswell, *Life of Johnson*, Oxford Standard Authors Edition (London, 1961), p. 438. Entry under 1770.
3. *The Anatomy of Melancholy* was first published in 1621, and was revised and enlarged in several subsequent editions. I use the edition of Floyd Dell and P. Jordan-Smith (London, 1930).
4. See André Du Laurens (Burton's "Laurentius"): "Love therefore having abused the eyes, as the proper spies and porters of the mind, maketh way for itselfe smoothly to glaunce along through the conducting guides, and passing without any perseverence in this sort through the veins unto the liver, doth suddenly imprint a burning desire to obtain the thing, which is or seemeth worthie to be beloved, setteth concupiscence on fire, and

beginneth by this desire all the strife and contention: but fearing herselfe too weake to encounter with reason, the principal part of the minde, she posteth in haste to the heart, to surprise and winne the same: whereof when she is once sure, as of the strongest holde, she afterwarde assaileth and setteth upon reason, and all the other principall powers of the minde so fiercely, as that she subdueth them, and maketh them her vassals and slaves." *A Discourse of the Preservation of the Sight: of Melancholic Diseases; of Rheums, and of Old Age,* trans. Richard Surphlet (London, 1599). Reprinted, Shakespeare Association Facsimile no. 15. London, 1938. P. 118.

[5] See *The Insatiate Countess,* II, i.

[6] Jacques Ferrand, *Erotomania, or a Treatise discoursing of the Essence, Causes, Symptomes, Prognosticks, and Cure of LOVE or Erotique Melancholy* (Oxford, 1640), p. 121.

[7] See Lawrence Babb, *The Elizabethan Malady* (East Lansing, 1951), p. 134.

[8] Du Laurens, p. 123.

[9] The symptom of searching a relative's countenance for a likeness to the beloved is elaborated in an interesting scene in *The Watsons.* Here the likeness becomes a subject of debate between the girl and her parents, who try to discourage her love by denying the resemblance:

> The discussion led to more intimate remarks, & Miss Edwardes gently asked Emma if she were not often reckoned very like her youngest brother.—Emma thought she could perceive a faint blush accompany the question, & there seemed something still more suspicious in the manner in which Mr E. took up the subject.—"You are paying Miss Emma no great compliment I think Mary, said he hastily—.... Mr. Watson!... Well, you astonish me.—There is not the least likeness in the world." (*MW,* 324)

[10] *Lamia,* 11. 189-190. Keats took the story of *Lamia* from the Love Melancholy section of *The Anatomy of Melancholy* (see p. 648); so he was himself steeped in the lore of love.

CHAPTER II: SURFACE AND SUBSURFACE

[1] A version of this paper was originally published in *ARIEL,* 5:2 (April, 1974), pp. 5-24. I am grateful to the editor for permission to reprint. Since then, further discussions of Jane Austen's handling of love and the passions have emerged. I refer the interested reader particularly to Barbara Hardy, "The Feelings and the Passions," the second chapter of her *A Reading of Jane Austen* (London, 1975), pp. 37-65, and Mark Kinkead-Weekes, "This Old Maid: Jane Austen replies to Charlotte Brontë and D. H. Lawrence," *Nineteenth-Century Fiction,* 30:3 (December, 1975), pp. 399-419. A. O. J. Cockshut's *Man and Woman: A Study of*

Love and the Novel, 1740-1940 (New York, 1978) emerged too recently for me to read it before my present text went to press.

[2] Letter to W. S. Williams, April 12, 1850. *The Shakespeare Head Brontë* (Oxford, 1931), xiv, p. 99. Reprinted in *Jane Austen: The Critical Heritage*, ed. B.C. Southam (London, 1968), p. 128.

[3] Letter to W. D. Howells, January 18, 1909. *Mark Twain's Letters*, ed. A. B. Paine, (New York, 1923), ii, p. 830.

[4] Unpublished manuscript entitled "Jane Austen." I quote from Ian Watt's introduction to *Jane Austen: a Collection of Critical Essays* (Englewood Cliffs, 1963), p. 7.

[5] "The Lady Novelists," *Westminster Review*, 58 (July, 1852), p. 134. See *Critical Heritage*, p. 140.

[6] Letter to Ruskin, November 5, 1855. *Letters of Elizabeth Barrett Browning*, ed. F. G. Kenyon, (London, 1897), ii, p. 217. See *Critical Heritage*, p. 25.

[7] *Jane Austen: a Collection of Critical Essays*, p. 4.

[8] Howard Babb has pointed out how "most of Jane Austen's critics are obsessed by a sense of her limitations." *Jane Austen's Novels: the Fabric of Dialogue* (Ohio, 1962), p. 3.

[9] "Biographical Notice" in her introduction to *Wuthering Heights*.

[10] The earlier novels have the most of this kind of traditional satire: General Tilney, Lucy Steele, and Caroline Bingley are deceitful; but Elizabeth, Mary Crawford, Emma and Captain Wentworth are self-deluded.

[11] Howard Babb has provided excellent analyses of these and other passages in *Jane Austen: the Fabric of Dialogue*. My emphasis differs from his, however.

[12] Lionel Trilling points out how Mary Crawford "cultivates the *style* of sensitivity, virtue, and intelligence." *The Opposing Self* (New York, 1955), p. 220.

[13] Marvin Mudrick comments perversely on this passage, "Mary has suddenly become Satan," and calls this final view of her "a grotesque makeshift." *Jane Austen: Irony as Defense and Discovery* (Princeton, 1952), p. 165. But the imagery throughout has prepared us for such a view of Mary.

[14] In "Apropos of *Lady Chatterley's Lover*" (1930). See Mark Kinkead-Weekes, cited above.

[15] *John Thomas and Lady Jane* (New York, 1972), p. 114.

[16] Scott was opposing this to what he called Jane Austen's "exquisite touch," and her "talent for describing the involvement and feelings and characters of ordinary life." *Journal of Walter Scott*, 1825-26 (London, 1939), ed. J. G. Tait, p. 135. See *Critical Heritage*, p. 106.

[17] *Jane Austen: Irony as Defense and Discovery*, p. 60.

[18] "On Some Forms of Irony in Literature," *Cornhill*, 58 (April, 1907), p. 499.

CHAPTER III: LOVE AND PEDAGOGY

[1] This was first published in *Jane Austen Today*, ed. Joel Weinsheimer (Athens, Ga., 1975); I am grateful to the University of Georgia Press for permission to reprint.

[2] The phrase is Pamela Hansford Johnson's. "The Sexual Life in Dickens's Novels," *Dickens 1970*, ed. Michael Slater (London, 1970), p. 179.

[3] *Sincerity and Authenticity* (London, 1972), p. 82. Professor Trilling elsewhere sardonically commented, "I know that pedagogy is a depressing subject to all persons of sensibility." "On the Teaching of Modern Literature," *Beyond Culture* (New York, 1965), p. 3.

[4] Geoffrey Gorer has explored this aspect of the novels in "The Myth in Jane Austen," *American Imago*, 2 (1941).

[5] See, for instance, David Smith, "Incest Patterns in two Victorian Novels," *Literature and Psychology*, 15:3 (Summer, 1965), pp. 135-162.

[6] See Gordon S. Haight, *George Eliot: a Biography* (Oxford, 1968), pp. 27, 49-50.

[7] *Sincerity and Authenticity*, p. 82.

[8] Unsigned review of James Austen-Leigh's *Memoir of Jane Austen* in the *North British Review* (April, 1870). Reprinted in *Jane Austen: The Critical Heritage*, ed. B. C. Southam (London, 1968), pp. 244 and 246.

[9] "Serious Reflections on *The Rise of the Novel*," *Novel: a Forum on Fiction*, I (1968), p. 218. Sylvia Myers has already challenged Professor Watt for this characteristic bit of swashbuckling in her article in the same journal, "Womanhood in Jane Austen's Novels," 3 (1970), pp. 225-232.

[10] See *Some Words of Jane Austen*, (Chicago, 1973), chapters 1 and 2.

[11] There is a similarity not only in the main plot, where hero and heroine come to accord only after having pointedly singled each other out for abuse, but also in the subplots—the making and breaking of the Hero/Claudio and Jane/Bingley matches being a point at fierce issue between the main characters. "God help the noble Claudio! If he have caught the Benedick, it will cost him a thousand pounds ere 'a be cured" (I, i), says Beatrice, and so might Elizabeth say of Bingley and Darcy. Hero's description of Beatrice, who "turns ... every man the wrong side out" (III, i), sounds like the unreformed Elizabeth:

> Disdain and scorn ride sparkling in her eyes,
> Misprising what they look on, and her wit
> Values itself so highly that to her
> All matter else seems weak. She cannot love ...
> She is so self-endeared.

And when Beatrice brings herself to love Benedick, she might be Elizabeth soliloquizing after talking to the housekeeper at Pemberley: "For others say thou dost deserve, and I / Believe it better than reportingly" (III, i). Darcy is obviously not so like Benedick. But he too is confident—as well he might be with Miss Bingley and Miss de Bourgh visibly eager to snap him up—that "It is certain I am loved of all ladies, only you excepted" (I, i). Benedick's determination that "till all graces be in one woman, one woman shall not come in my grace" (II, iii) is echoed in Darcy's exacting notions of what constitutes accomplishment in a woman. And when it comes to the point, Benedick, like Darcy, finds it difficult to express himself warmly and captivatingly: "No, I was not born under a rhyming planet, nor I cannot woo in festival terms" (V, ii). Amen to that, Elizabeth at Hunsford might well have agreed!

12 Cf. Lloyd W. Brown: "The myth of the asexual Jane Austen novel is more revealing of our surfeited twentieth-century 'senses' than it is of Jane Austen's work." "Jane Austen and the Feminist Tradition," *Nineteenth-Century Fiction*, 28:3 (1973), p. 333.

13 I use Chapman's edition of the play, included with his edition of *Mansfield Park*.

14 See Arnold Kettle's section on *Emma* in *An Introduction to the English Novel* (London, 1951).

15 I refer to his essay of 1921, "The Metaphysical Poets," reprinted in *Collected Essays* (London, 1932).

CHAPTER IV: LOVE AND MARRIAGE

1 See, for example, Mark Schorer, "Pride Unprejudiced," *Kenyon Review* 18 (Winter, 1956), 72-91, and Lloyd W. Brown, "The Business of Marrying and Mothering," in *Jane Austen's Achievement*, ed. Juliet McMaster (London, 1976), 27-43.

2 See Schorer, above, p. 85.

3 See Alice Munro's short story, "An Ounce of Cure," in which the narrator sees her ex-boyfriend play the role of Darcy in the school's production of *Pride and Prejudice*: "I was overcome with pain and delight at the sight of Mr. Darcy in white breeches, silk waistcoat and sideburns. It was surely seeing Martin as Darcy that did for me; every girl is in love with Darcy anyway, and the part gave Martin an arrogance and male splendour in my eyes." *Dance of the Happy Shades* (Toronto, 1968), p. 76.

4 I have discussed this element in Crawford elsewhere, in "The Continuity of Jane Austen's Novels," *Studies in English Literature*, 10:4 (Autumn, 1970), p. 732.

5 See Marjorie Proops, *Pride Prejudice and Proops* (London, 1975), p. 12.

6 *Changing Places* (London, 1975), p. 195. I am grateful to the publishers, Martin Secker & Warburg Ltd., and to the American distributors, Curtis Brown Ltd., for permission to quote.

www.ingramcontent.com/pod-product-compliance
Lightning Source LLC
Chambersburg PA
CBHW060345050426
42449CB00011B/2847